INDIANA
COOK BOOK

D1412444

GOLDEN WEST ✹ PUBLISHERS

Front cover photo courtesy Shoup's Country Foods, Inc.
Back cover photo (left) *Indiana State Fair courtesy Indiana State Fair Board*
Back cover photo (right) *University of Notre Dame courtesy L. K. Dunn/Notre Dame Photographic*

ISBN – 1-885590-57-1

Printed in the United States of America

Copyright © 2001, by Golden West Publishers. All rights reserved. This book or any portion thereof may not be reproduced in any form, except for review purposes, without the written permission of the publisher.

Information in this book is deemed to be authentic and accurate by publisher. However, publisher disclaims any liability incurred in connection with the use of information appearing in this book.

Golden West Publishers, Inc.
4113 N. Longview Ave.
Phoenix, AZ 85014, USA
(602) 265-4392

Visit our website: http://www.goldenwestpublishers.com

★ ★ ★ ★ ★ *Indiana Cook Book* ★ ★ ★ ★ ★

Table of Contents

★ ★ ★ ★ ★ *Indiana Cook Book* ★ ★ ★ ★ ★

Table of Contents *(Continued)*

Introduction

Experience the Hoosier State from berry patches to onion farms and persimmon orchards to corn fields when you sample these culinary creations from the state of Indiana. The **Indiana Cook Book** offers a myriad of worldly delights and down home treats.

Feast on favorites from *Old-Fashioned Chicken and Dumplings* to *Currant Glazed Duckling with Apple-Walnut Stuffing* and *Raspberry Truffle Brownies* to *Persimmon Pudding*. Indulge in a *Turnip Salad* with vegetables fresh from the garden, revel in savory *Baked Salmon with Cheese Sauce* from the waters of Lake Michigan, or tempt your sweet tooth with an authentic Amish *Shoofly Pie*.

In addition to charming recipes that complement Indiana's rich American history, the **Indiana Cook Book** features notable information and trivia about the state's celebrated Hoosier heritage. Savor these wonderful foods that accent the rural agricultural regions and urban metropolitan communities; they are the tradition and diversity of Indiana.

Whatever your craving, a collection of mouth-watering dishes awaits you!

Indiana Facts

Size – 38th largest state with an area of 35,867 square miles
Population – 6,080,485
State Capital – Indianapolis
Statehood – Dec. 11, 1816, the 19th state
    admitted to the Union
State Nickname – The Hoosier State
State Song – "On the Banks of the Wabash,
    Far Away," by Paul Dresser
State Motto – *The Crossroads of America*
State River – Wabash River
State Bird – Cardinal
State Stone – Salem Limestone
State Poem – "Indiana"
    by Arthur Franklin Mapes

State Tree
Tulip Tree

State Flower
Peony

Famous Hoosiers

George Ade, *humorist;* Leon Ames, *actor;* Larry Bird, *basketball star;* Bill Blass, *fashion designer;* Frank Borman, *astronaut;* Hoagy Carmichael, *jazz musician;* John Chapman, *Johnny Appleseed;* Jim Davis, *Garfield cartoonist;* James Dean, *actor;* Theodore Dreiser, *author;* Jeff Gordon, *race car driver;* Gus Grissom, *astronaut;* Benjamin Harrison, *23rd president;* Jimmy Hoffa, *union leader;* Michael Jackson, *entertainer;* Alfred C. Kinsey, *zoologist;* David Letterman, *comedian;* Eli Lilly, *businessman;* Abraham Lincoln, *16th president;* Carole Lombard, *actress;* Shelley Long, *actress;* James McCracken, *tenor;* Steve McQueen, *actor;* Joaquin Miller, *poet;* Meredith Nicholson, *novelist / diplomat;* Paul Osborn, *playwright;* Jane Pauley, *broadcaster / journalist;* Cole Porter, *composer;* Ernie Pyle, *journalist;* James Whitcomb Riley, *poet;* Knute Rockne, *football coach;* Rex Stout, *mystery writer;* Red Skelton, *comedian;* Booth Tarkington, *author;* Twyla Tharp, *choreographer;* Forrest Tucker, *actor;* Kurt Vonnegut, *author;* Lewis Wallace, *author;* Wendell Wilkie, *lawyer.*

Indiana Visitor Information: 1-800-289-6646

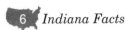

Appetizers

Stuffed Mushroom Caps

"For three generations, our family has been proud to be a progressive part of the Schererville Community. Seventy years have brought vast changes in our ways of life...what has not changed is the spirit and desire of the Teibel family to provide our guests with the finest quality of food and service."

Robert Teibel—Teibel's Restaurant, Schererville

1 cup shredded SWISS CHEESE
1 cup shredded CHEDDAR CHEESE
1 cup shredded AMERICAN CHEESE
1/8 cup BACON BITS
1/8 cup chopped GREEN ONIONS
16-18 MUSHROOM CAPS
SALT and PEPPER

Preheat oven to 350°. Mix all cheeses, bacon bits and green onions together in a mixing bowl. Parboil the mushroom caps until medium soft and allow to drain until as dry as possible. Arrange the mushroom caps bottom up, on a lightly buttered baking tray and season with salt and pepper to taste. Cover the mushroom caps completely with the cheese mixture. Bake for 15 minutes or until all cheese is melted.

Serves 2-3.

Kielbasa Appetizer

"This is a family favorite."

Frances K. Idzik—Schererville

1 lb. KIELBASA, cut into 1/4-inch thick slices
1 cup MAPLE SYRUP
1 cup GINGER ALE

In a 13 x 9 baking pan, arrange kielbasa slices in a single layer. Pour maple syrup and ginger ale over the top. Bake at 250° for 2 hours; turn slices once after the first hour. Remove kielbasa from baking pan, add toothpicks and serve.

Sensational Salsa

"This is a great way to use fresh vegetables."

Deborah Reed—Columbia City

5 lbs. ROMA TOMATOES, blanched and peeled
3 BELL PEPPERS, chopped
3 Tbsp. fresh DILL
2 Tbsp. GARLIC POWDER
1 Tbsp. OREGANO
6 JALAPEÑO PEPPERS, chopped
3 lg. ONIONS, chopped
3 cups chopped CHIVES
2 tsp. CAYENNE
1 Tbsp. BASIL
2 cans (6 oz. ea.) TOMATO PASTE, optional
1 cup SUGAR

In a 5-quart saucepan, combine tomato "meat" and all remaining ingredients, except the sugar. Bring mixture to a boil, reduce heat and simmer for 20 minutes or until vegetables are tender. Add sugar and blend well. If the salsa needs thickening, add more tomato paste as needed. Place in blender or food processor and blend to desired consistency. Pour salsa into hot, sterilized jars and seal. Serve with chips for a great appetizer.

Party Cheeseball

"Serve this with crackers for a great appetizer."

Ruth Ann Mast—Bremen

1 pkg. (8 oz.) CREAM CHEESE, room temperature
1 jar (5 oz.) CHEESE SPREAD
1/8 tsp. GARLIC POWDER
1 tsp. WORCESTERSHIRE SAUCE
1-2 Tbsp. soft BUTTER
1/8 lb. DRIED BEEF, chopped fine
1/4 cup chopped PECANS
1/4 cup chopped dried PARSLEY

Combine all ingredients together thoroughly (except pecans and parsley). Form into a ball and chill for 8 hours or overnight. When well-chilled, roll in pecans and parsley.

Batter Up!
The first professional baseball game was played in Fort Wayne on May 4, 1871.

Blue Cheese Mushrooms

"This is a very tasty treat."

Patricia L. Green—Fort Wayne

12-14 lg. MUSHROOMS
1/4 cup BUTTER
1/4 cup minced GREEN ONIONS
1/4 cup crumbled BLUE CHEESE
2 Tbsp. fine BREAD CRUMBS
SALT and PEPPER
3 Tbsp. coarse BREAD CRUMBS

Preheat oven to 350°. Mince mushroom stems. In a small skillet, melt butter and sauté mushroom stems and green onions. Stir in cheese and fine bread crumbs. Season with salt and pepper to taste. Stuff mushroom caps with mixture and place on a baking sheet. Top caps with coarse bread crumbs and bake for 12 minutes.

Meatballs Florentine

"Deb Perry of Bluffton won first place in our Appetizers and Dips contest with this recipe in 1992."

Deb Osa—American Dairy Association of Indiana, Indianapolis

Meatballs:
- 1 lb. lean GROUND CHUCK
- 1 cup large curd COTTAGE CHEESE
- 1/4 cup grated PARMESAN CHEESE
- 1/2 cup finely chopped ONION
- 1 EGG
- 1 pkg. (10 oz.) frozen chopped SPINACH, defrosted and well-drained
- 1/2 tsp. SALT
- 1/4 tsp. PEPPER
- 1 clove GARLIC, minced

Sauce:
- 2 BEEF BOUILLON CUBES
- 1/4 cup DRY RED WINE
- 2 cups BOILING WATER
- 2 Tbsp. CORNSTARCH

In a large mixing bowl, combine all meatball ingredients and mix well. Form into 24 balls approximately 1-inch in diameter. Bake at 450° in a lightly buttered 13 x 9 pan for 20 minutes. In another bowl, blend together all sauce ingredients. Push meatballs aside and scrape out drippings. Rearrange meatballs and pour sauce over all. Reduce heat to 350° and bake for 30 minutes longer. Serve in a hot chafing dish or crock pot.

Serves 10-12.

Indianapolis

This city, the largest in Indiana, ranks as one of the chief centers of manufacturing, transportation and the distribution of goods in the Midwest. Situated in the center of Indiana, Indianapolis is sometimes called the "Crossroads of America" because many routes of highway and railroad traffic meet here. Worldwide attention is focused here when the famous Indianapolis 500 automobile race is held on Memorial Day weekend.

Shrimp Dip

"I have had this recipe for years!"

Paula Teibel—Hammond

1 pkg. (8 oz.) CREAM CHEESE
1 can (10.75 oz.) CREAM OF SHRIMP SOUP
1 pkg. (1 oz.) unflavored GELATIN
1 can (4.25 oz.) SHRIMP, drained
1 sm. ONION, diced
1 cup MAYONNAISE

In a medium saucepan, heat cream cheese and soup, stirring constantly until heated through; allow to cool. In a small bowl, combine 1/4 cup of the soup mixture with the gelatin and mix well; pour back into the soup mixture. Add remaining ingredients and stir well. Pour into a serving bowl and chill until ready to serve. Serve with vegetable crackers.

Corydon

Corydon was Indiana's first state capital (1816-1825). Indiana's only official civil war battle took place here in 1863.

Finger Lickin' Chicken Wings

"An all-time family favorite."

Frances K. Idzik—Schererville

4 lbs. CHICKEN WINGS

Marinade:
1 cup SOY SAUCE	1 tsp. GARLIC SALT
1 cup SUGAR	1/4 cup VEGETABLE OIL
1 tsp. GINGER	1/4 cup PINEAPPLE JUICE

Cut wings into three parts; discarding the tips. Arrange wings in a shallow glass dish. In a bowl, combine marinade ingredients and mix well. Pour over wings; cover and marinate in the refrigerator overnight. Remove wings from marinade, place in a 13 x 9 baking pan and bake at 350° for 1 1/2 hours.

Bar-B-Que Dipping Sauce

"This is a favorite for french fries, chicken strips or bite-size pieces of pork or beef. Kids love it!"

Ruth Ann Mast—Bremen

2 cups KETCHUP
3/4 cup packed BROWN SUGAR
1 Tbsp. YELLOW MUSTARD
6 Tbsp. WORCESTERSHIRE SAUCE
1/4 cup LIQUID SMOKE
2 Tbsp. HONEY
3-4 drops TABASCO®
    or 1/8 tsp. CAYENNE, optional

Combine all ingredients thoroughly, cover and refrigerate until ready to serve.

Did You Know?

More than 3,600 Amish operate farms in the Berne area. On shopping days, their horses and buggies can be seen at hitching posts throughout this city.

Taffy Apple Dip

"This recipe was submitted by Leah J. Gerber from Barbara Schwartz's 'Amish Cooking Vol. 2.' cookbook."

Kris Cisney—Berne Chamber of Commerce, Berne

1 pkg. (8 oz.) CREAM CHEESE, softened
3/4 cup packed BROWN SUGAR
1 Tbsp. VANILLA
1/2 cup chopped PEANUTS
6 APPLES, cut into wedges

In a small bowl, beat cream cheese, brown sugar and vanilla until smooth. Spread mixture on a small serving plate and top with nuts. Serve with apple wedges on the side.

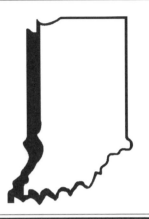

Breakfast & Brunch

Trolley Cafe Baked Oatmeal

"If you like oatmeal, you'll love this unique variation. This is a popular recipe in our Midwest area and a favorite of our cafe customers."

Aaron and Mary Jane Hoober—Trolley Cafe, Goshen

1/2 cup MARGARINE or VEGETABLE OIL*
1 cup packed BROWN SUGAR
2 EGGS
2 Tbsp. BAKING POWDER
1 cup MILK
3 cups OATMEAL
1 tsp. SALT

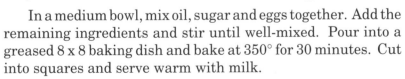

In a medium bowl, mix oil, sugar and eggs together. Add the remaining ingredients and stir until well-mixed. Pour into a greased 8 x 8 baking dish and bake at 350° for 30 minutes. Cut into squares and serve warm with milk.

*For low-fat version, use 1/2 cup of applesauce in place of margarine or oil.

Grandmother Reagan's Waffles

"This was my grandmother Virgie Reagan's recipe and is our family's very favorite."

Barb Fausett—Frankfort

5 cups FLOUR
4 tsp. BAKING POWDER
4 EGGS, separated
4 tsp. SUGAR

4 cups MILK
1 cup BUTTER or
    MARGARINE, melted

In a large mixing bowl, sift flour and baking powder together. Add egg yolks, sugar, milk and butter and stir well. In another bowl, beat the egg whites until stiff, then fold into the batter. Bake on a hot waffle iron until golden brown.

Crumb Coffee Cake

"This recipe was passed down to me by my grandmother. She is the one who taught me to cook."

Sara M. Tracy—Greenwood

2 cups FLOUR
1 tsp. CINNAMON
1 cup packed BROWN
    SUGAR
1/2 cup MARGARINE
1/2 tsp. SALT
1 tsp. BAKING POWDER

1 EGG, beaten
1 cup SOUR MILK*
1 tsp. BAKING SODA
1 tsp. VANILLA
1/2 cup RAISINS
1/2 cup NUTS

In a bowl, combine flour, cinnamon, sugar and margarine until crumbly. Set aside 1/2 cup of flour mixture for topping. Stir in salt, baking powder and egg. In a separate bowl, combine sour milk and baking soda and stir until foamy. Pour sour milk mixture into flour mixture and add vanilla; mix well. Fold in raisins and nuts. Pour mixture into a greased 8 x 8 cake pan and sprinkle with remaining topping mixture and additional cinnamon. Bake at 350° for 40-45 minutes.

*Note: For sour milk, combine 1 cup milk and 1 tsp. vinegar.

Oliver Inn
Breakfast Delight

"This recipe was given to me by a fellow innkeeper who got it from one of her guests. It is my very favorite and gets rave reviews from all of our guests."

Venera Monahan—The Oliver Inn Bed & Breakfast, South Bend

1 pkg. (10 oz.) frozen chopped SPINACH
6 EGGS, unbeaten
2 lbs. COTTAGE CHEESE, well-drained
2 cups grated SHARP CHEDDAR CHEESE
1/3 cup FLOUR
6 tsp. chopped GREEN ONIONS

Defrost spinach and bring all ingredients to room temperature. Place in a large mixer bowl in order listed. Mix thoroughly at medium speed for three minutes (mixture will be lumpy). Pour batter into a greased 13 x 9 baking pan. Bake at 350° for 45-60 minutes or until top is golden brown and a knife inserted in the middle comes out clean. Let stand for 10 minutes before cutting into squares. May be frozen after baking. If frozen, heat in moderate oven for 15-20 minutes before serving.

Refrigerator Bran Muffins

"The smell of these muffins cooking is a wonderful aroma for our guests as they wake up, and they go well with our hearty country breakfasts."

Treva Swarm—Bee Hive Bed & Breakfast, Middlebury

1 pkg. (10 oz.) RAISIN BRAN CEREAL
5 cups FLOUR
5 tsp. BAKING SODA
2 tsp. SALT

3 cups SUGAR
1 qt. BUTTERMILK
1 cup VEGETABLE OIL
4 EGGS, beaten

Mix all ingredients together until moistened. Store in covered container in refrigerator until ready to bake. Fill muffin tins 3/4 full and bake at 350° for 15-20 minutes.

Potato-Cheese Strata

"This is a much requested recipe at our inn."

Tammy Schaffer—The Washington Street Inn, Bluffton

1 1/2 lbs. frozen HASH BROWN POTATOES, thawed
2 Tbsp. BUTTER
1/2 cup chopped GREEN ONIONS
2/3 cup condensed CREAM OF MUSHROOM SOUP
2/3 cup MILK
1 1/2 cups SOUR CREAM
4 cups shredded COLBY-JACK or CHEDDAR CHEESE
8 EGGS
1/2 tsp. TABASCO®
1/4 tsp. SALT
15 slices BACON, cooked and crumbled
FRESH FRUIT for garnish

Spread potatoes in a casserole dish and bake in a 250° oven for 1 hour. When potatoes are done, melt butter in a skillet and sauté green onions until tender. In a large bowl, combine all ingredients except bacon and mix well. Turn into a 3-quart glass baking dish that has been sprayed with cooking spray.* Bake at 350° for 1 hour. Sprinkle crumbled bacon over the top 10 minutes before the end of baking time. Let casserole stand for 5 minutes before cutting into serving portions. (You can use a quiche pan and cut into wedges). Garnish with fresh fruit.

Serves 6-8.

*Strata may be made in advance, covered and refrigerated. When ready to bake, add 10-15 minutes to baking time.

The National Road

Now U.S. 40, the road from Cumberland, Maryland to Vandalia, Illinois was completed across Indiana from Richmond to Terre Haute about 1850.

Sausage & Eggs

"My daughter gave me this delicious breakfast recipe."

Patricia L. Green—Fort Wayne

1 lb. SAUSAGE
6 EGGS, beaten
2 cups MILK
1 tsp. DRY MUSTARD

2 slices BREAD, torn into
   small pieces
1 cup grated CHEDDAR
   CHEESE

In a large skillet, brown sausage; drain well. In a mixing bowl, combine eggs, milk, mustard and bread. Stir in cheese and sausage. Pour mixture into a greased 11 x 7 baking dish, cover and refrigerate overnight. Bake at 350° for 45 minutes.

Mom's
Sour Cream Coffee Cake

"This recipe was given to my mother by a dear friend many years ago. It never fails to please my guests."

Joanie Rumple—Farmhouse Bed & Breakfast, Dana

1 cup SUGAR
1 stick BUTTER, softened
2 EGGS
1 cup SOUR CREAM
2 cups sifted FLOUR

1 tsp. BAKING SODA
1 tsp. BAKING POWDER
Dash of SALT
1 tsp. VANILLA

Topping:
   1/3 cup packed BROWN SUGAR
   1/4 cup SUGAR
   1 tsp. CINNAMON
   1 cup finely chopped PECANS

In a large mixing bowl, cream together sugar and butter, adding eggs one at a time. Mix in sour cream. Fold in flour, baking soda, baking powder and salt. Add vanilla and mix well. In a separate bowl, combine topping ingredients and mix well. Pour half of the batter in a greased 9 x 9 pan. Sprinkle half of the topping on batter. Add remaining batter and sprinkle with remaining topping. Bake at 325° for 40-45 minutes.

Peculiar
Cinnamon Pancakes

"I received this recipe from my sister-in-law. It tastes like a cross between French toast and pancakes. Served with bacon, coffee and juice, it makes a quick and tasty breakfast."

Laura McInturf—Elkhart

1/2 cup MILK	1/2 stick BUTTER or
1/2 cup FLOUR	MARGARINE
2 EGGS, slightly beaten	CINNAMON

In a bowl, mix milk and flour together; add eggs and stir well. Heat butter in an 8-inch glass pie plate until bubbly. Pour batter into the pie plate and sprinkle generously with cinnamon. Bake at 425° for 15-20 minutes.

Blueberry Coffee Cake

"A favorite breakfast treat on our farm."

Shiela DeBoer—Eenigenburg Blueberry Farm, Demotte

3/4 cup SUGAR	2 tsp. BAKING POWDER
1/4 cup MARGARINE	1/2 tsp. LEMON JUICE
1 EGG	1 1/2 cups BLUEBERRIES
1/2 cup MILK	1/2 tsp. SALT
2 cups FLOUR	

Mix all ingredients together and spread in a greased 9 x 9 baking pan. Spread **Cinnamon Topping** over batter and bake at 375° for 25-35 minutes or until tests done.

Cinnamon Topping

1/2 cup SUGAR	1/2 tsp. CINNAMON
1/3 cup FLOUR	1/4 cup melted MARGARINE

Combine all ingredients well.

Orange Oatmeal Pecan Pancakes

"This is a delightful recipe!"

Rosalind Slabaugh—Spring View Bed & Breakfast, Goshen

1 1/2 cups QUICK-COOKING OATS	1 cup MILK
1 cup FLOUR	1 cup ORANGE JUICE
3 Tbsp. SUGAR, optional	2 EGGS
1 tsp. SALT	1/2 cup chopped PECANS
2 1/2 tsp. BAKING POWDER	OIL for frying
1/3 cup OIL	

Combine all ingredients (except oil) in a large bowl, mix well, cover and refrigerate overnight. In a large skillet, heat oil, pour in 1/4 cup of batter for each pancake; fry until golden brown on both sides.

Yields 12-14 (3-inch) pancakes.

Did You Know?

Elwood Haynes of Kokomo preceded Ford by designing one of the first successful gasoline-powered cars in 1894.

Indiana Biscuits & Gravy

"This makes a hearty breakfast whether served alone or with eggs and hash browns."

Joann D. Saine—Auburn

1 lb. seasoned bulk PORK SAUSAGE	Dash of TABASCO®
3 Tbsp. FLOUR	SALT
2 cups MILK	BISCUITS

In a heavy skillet, crumble sausage and cook slowly over low heat, stirring occasionally until browned; drain. Sprinkle flour over meat and stir well. Gradually add milk, stirring constantly; continue to cook until mixture boils gently and thickens. Add Tabasco and salt to taste. Serve over warm biscuits.

Streusel Kuchen
(Coffee Cake)

"This was my German grandmother's recipe. It has been handed down through the years."

Tammy Schaffer—The Washington Street Inn, Bluffton

Cake:

3/4 cup SUGAR	1 1/2 cups FLOUR
1/4 cup SHORTENING	1/2 tsp. SALT
1 EGG	2 tsp. BAKING POWDER
1/2 cup MILK	

Streusel:

1/2 cup BROWN SUGAR	2 Tbsp. melted BUTTER
2 tsp. CINNAMON	1/2 cup chopped PECANS
2 Tbsp. FLOUR	

In a bowl, combine sugar, shortening and egg; stir in milk. Sift flour and mix with salt and baking powder. Combine mixtures. In another bowl, combine all streusel ingredients; mix well. Spread 1/2 of the batter in a 9-inch round baking pan that has been greased and floured. Sprinkle with half of the streusel mixture. Add remaining batter and sprinkle with remaining streusel mixture. Bake at 350° for 25-30 minutes or until a toothpick inserted in the middle comes out clean.

Corn Griddle Cakes

"This was my grandmother's recipe."

Bonnie L. Domer—Bristol

1 cup CORNMEAL	1 EGG
1/4 cup FLOUR	1 cup MILK
3 tsp. BAKING POWDER	2 Tbsp. OIL
1/2 tsp. SALT	OIL for frying

Sift dry ingredients into a medium mixing bowl. In a large mixing bowl, beat together egg, milk and 2 tablespoons oil. Add flour mixture and beat until smooth; batter should pour from a spoon. In a skillet or on a hot griddle, heat oil, pour 1/4 cup of batter into oil and fry until golden brown on both sides.

Soups & Salads

Cheesy Bacon Potato Soup

"A Christmas Eve family favorite! This can be served with cheese and crackers, veggies and dip and a dessert for a great light meal before the Christmas Day feast."

Dotti Thomas—Frankfort

6-8 slices BACON
1 sm. ONION, diced
2 CARROTS, shredded
6-7 med. POTATOES, diced
1/2 cup BUTTER
3/4 cup FLOUR
4 cups MILK
1 (8 oz.) jar CHEESE WHIZ®

In a large skillet, fry bacon until crisp and then drain, reserving 3 tablespoons of drippings. In a saucepan, cook onion, carrots and potatoes in just enough water to cover them; do not drain. Add bacon drippings and stir. In a medium saucepan, melt butter, then add flour, milk and Cheese Whiz; stir until smooth and thick. Pour over cooked vegetables and stir together. Crumble the bacon and sprinkle over the top.

Chicken & Apple Stew

Indiana State Poultry Association—West Lafayette

1 CHICKEN, cut into parts
1/2 tsp. NUTMEG
1/2 tsp. SALT
1/4 tsp. PEPPER
2 tsp. DIJON MUSTARD
1 3/4 cups warm, low sodium
   CHICKEN BROTH

1/4 cup APPLE CIDER VINEGAR
6 WHOLE CLOVES
3 CARROTS, peeled and sliced
6 APPLES, peeled and sliced
1 cup shredded CABBAGE
1 cup APPLESAUCE

Spray a large Dutch oven with vegetable cooking spray and heat over medium-high temperature. Add chicken and cook, about 10 minutes, turning to brown on all sides. Sprinkle with nutmeg, salt and pepper. Spread mustard over chicken pieces; add warm broth, vinegar, cloves and carrots; bring to a boil. Cover, reduce heat to low and cook 15 minutes. Add apples and cook 5 minutes. Add cabbage, stirring into liquid. Cook, covered, about 10 minutes more or until fork can be inserted in chicken with ease. With a slotted spoon, remove chicken and vegetables to a warm serving bowl and keep warm. Stir applesauce into remaining broth; boil on high temperature for 5 minutes and pour over chicken and vegetables.

Overnight Slaw

Nancye Barnhart—Brown County Pioneer Museum, Nashville

2 tsp. SALT
1 cup WATER
4 cups shredded CABBAGE

1 GREEN BELL PEPPER,
   chopped
2 stalks CELERY, chopped

In a bowl, combine salt and water. Add cabbage and bell pepper and let stand for 1 hour. Drain or squeeze out liquid; add celery to bowl. Pour *Slaw Marinade* over all, cover tightly and let stand overnight.

Slaw Marinade

1 cup SUGAR
1/2 cup WHITE VINEGAR

1/2 cup WATER
1 tsp. MUSTARD SEED

In a saucepan, combine all ingredients. Bring to a boil; cool.

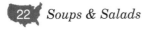

Country Potato Soup

"This is a special family recipe."

Rosannah E. Shaw—Elkhart

3 cups pared and diced POTATOES	1/2 tsp. SALT
1/2 cup diced CELERY	2 cups MILK, divided
1/2 cup diced ONIONS	1 cup SOUR CREAM
1 1/2 cups WATER	2 Tbsp. FLOUR
2 CHICKEN BOUILLON CUBES	1 tsp. chopped CHIVES

In a large saucepan, mix together potatoes, celery, onions, water, bouillon cubes and salt. Cover and simmer 20 minutes or until potatoes are just tender. Add 1 cup of the milk; reheat. In a medium bowl, combine sour cream, flour, chives and remaining milk; mix well. Gradually stir sour cream mixture into potato mixture and continue to simmer over low heat, stirring until thickened.

Easy Creamy Broccoli Soup

Wilma Boyer—Indiana State Fair, Indianapolis

1 pkg. (10 oz.) frozen chopped BROCCOLI
2 cups MILK
2 Tbsp. BUTTER
1 cup POTATO FLAKES
2 tsp. MINCED ONION
1 cup CHICKEN BROTH
1/2 tsp. SALT

Cook broccoli according to package directions, omitting salt. Put undrained broccoli in blender container. In a saucepan, heat milk and butter (do not boil). Stir in potato flakes and onion. Add milk mixture to broccoli and process briefly. Return to saucepan; add broth and salt. Simmer 10 minutes on low heat.

Makes 3 cups.

Amish Acres Bean Soup

"This soup is the first course of the Threshers Dinner that we have been serving in our century-old barn restaurant for 30 years."

Angie Pletcher Stillson—Amish Acres, Nappanee

1 lb. mixed DRIED BEANS*
1 HAM BONE
1/2 cup chopped ONION
1/2 tsp. SEASONING SALT

1/2 tsp. CELERY SALT
Dash of GARLIC SALT
SALT and PEPPER

Soak beans in water overnight. Drain, add fresh water and cook slowly with the ham bone for 2 hours. Add onion, seasoning salt, celery salt and garlic salt. Add salt and pepper to taste. Remove ham bone, trim off any meat and return ham bone to pot. Add ham bits and simmer for 1 hour.

*Great Northern, navy, pinto, lima, black, etc.

Did You Know?

The first official airmail flight by the U. S. Postal Service was made by Professor John Wise and his balloon, "Jupiter," in Lafayette—August, 1859.

Carrot-Pineapple Salad

"This is a salad my mother always served when she had company. We included this favorite in our family cook book."

Esther H. Goodwin—Noblesville

2 pkgs. (3 oz. ea.) LEMON JELL-O®
2 cups BOILING WATER
1 cup chopped CARROTS

1 can (20 oz.) CRUSHED
PINEAPPLE
1/2 cup COLD WATER

In a medium mixing bowl, dissolve Jell-O in boiling water. Stir in carrots, crushed pineapple and pineapple juice. Add cold water and stir. Pour into gelatin mold or serving bowl and refrigerate until firm.

Tomato Cups

"This dish is especially great with fresh garden tomatoes!"

Sherrill Boggs—Columbia City

4 lg. ripe TOMATOES
3 HARD-BOILED EGGS, chopped
1 sm. CUCUMBER, diced
4 GREEN ONIONS, diced
1/2 cup diced CELERY
1/2 cup MAYONNAISE
1 Tbsp. VINEGAR
1 Tbsp. SUGAR
1 Tbsp. WATER
SALT and PEPPER
LETTUCE
Fresh PARSLEY for garnish

Cut off tops of tomatoes; scoop out pulp and place it in a strainer. Turn the shells upside down on paper towels to drain. In a medium bowl, mix together eggs, cucumber, onions and celery. Add strained tomato pulp to the mixture. In a small bowl, mix together mayonnaise, vinegar, sugar and water. Add salt and pepper to taste. Combine mixtures and stir well. Spoon mixture into tomato shells and refrigerate for at least 2 hours. Serve on a bed of lettuce leaves and garnish with parsley.

Fort Wayne

The St. Mary's and St. Joseph rivers join within this city to form the Maumee River. In 1832, the construction of the Wabash and Erie Canal brought many Irish and German immigrant workers to the area and the city flourished. Fort Wayne is known as "The City of Attractions" with numerous museums and historic sites, one of which is the Johnny Appleseed Park where John Chapman, better known as Johnny Appleseed, is buried.

Strawberry-Rhubarb Salad

"I received this recipe a long time ago from a very good friend of the family and have passed it along to others over the years."

Viola Ayers Collins—Lebanon

4 cups chopped RHUBARB
1 1/2 cups SUGAR
1/2 cup WATER
1 can (8 oz.) CRUSHED PINEAPPLE
1 pkg. (10 oz.) frozen, sweetened
    STRAWBERRIES
Dash of SALT
1 pkg. (3 oz.) STRAWBERRY JELL-O®
1/2 cup chopped PECANS
WHIPPED CREAM

In a large saucepan, combine all ingredients except Jell-O, pecans and whipped cream. Cook over medium heat until rhubarb is tender. Add Jell-O and pecans. Pour into mold or serving bowl and chill until firm. Top with whipped cream.

Apricot Salad

"Jell-O salads show up at family gatherings, church events and club meetings. They are a part of Indiana meals."

Wilhelmina Burket—Lafayette

1 pkg. (6 oz.) APRICOT JELL-O®
1 can (16 oz.) CRUSHED PINEAPPLE, drained, juice reserved
1/2 cup BOILING WATER
1 lg. jar (6 oz.) APRICOT BABY FOOD
1 pkg. (8 oz.) CREAM CHEESE, softened
1/2 cup chopped PECANS (optional)
1 ctn. (8 oz.) COOL WHIP®

In a medium mixing bowl, dissolve Jell-O in pineapple juice and boiling water; allow to cool slightly. Stir in pineapple, apricot baby food, cream cheese and pecans; blend in Cool Whip. Refrigerate until thoroughly chilled.

Strawberry-Spinach Salad

"This recipe is from my mother. We have been growing fruits and vegetables on our farm since 1926."

Beverly Huber Engleman—Joe Huber Family Farm & Restaurant, Starlight

Fresh SPINACH, torn into pieces
1 pt. fresh STRAWBERRIES, sliced
TOASTED ALMONDS

Place spinach on salad plates, add strawberries and top with almonds. Pour *Wine Vinegar Dressing* over salad just before serving.

Wine Vinegar Dressing

1/2 cup SUGAR
1 tsp. DRY MUSTARD
1 tsp. SALT
1/2 tsp. CELERY SEED

3 Tbsp. grated ONION
1 cup VEGETABLE OIL
1/3 cup WINE VINEGAR

In a small bowl, blend sugar, mustard, salt, celery seed and onion. Gradually add oil and vinegar, beating constantly. Refrigerate for several hours.

Turnip Salad

"Area garden shops have contests and the avid gardeners in our area take pride in growing the largest, longest or heaviest vegetables. Summertime brings the weekend farmers' markets and many roadside stands that sell beautiful homegrown garden goodies."

Martha Molebash—Elkhart

3 cups shredded TURNIPS
1/2 cup RAISINS
1 Tbsp. LEMON JUICE

1 cup shredded CARROTS
1 cup MAYONNAISE

In a large mixing bowl, combine all ingredients; mix well. Chill for at least 1 hour.

Carol's Chicken Salad

"As a 'lazy cook' in a family of great cooks, I found this recipe was not only very easy, but also impressed even my grandmother who had grown up cooking for farm hands and family."

Carol J. Carr—Edinburgh

4 CHICKEN BREASTS, cooked, deboned and diced
1 Tbsp. minced ONION
2 cups halved and seeded WHITE GRAPES
1 can (11 oz.) MANDARIN ORANGES, cut into pieces
1/2 cup SLIVERED ALMONDS
MAYONNAISE
LEMON JUICE

In a medium salad bowl, combine chicken, onion, grapes, oranges and almonds. Stir in enough mayonnaise to moisten, sprinkle with lemon juice and mix thoroughly. Cover and refrigerate until ready to serve.

Overnight Lettuce Salad

Nancye Barnhart—Brown County Pioneer Museum, Nashville

1 head LETTUCE
1/2 cup chopped CELERY
1 bunch GREEN ONIONS, chopped
1 cup sliced WATER CHESTNUTS
1 pkg. frozen GREEN PEAS, thawed
1 cup shredded MONTEREY JACK CHEESE
2 cups MAYONNAISE
2 tsp. SUGAR
Dash of CRAZY SALT® or MRS. DASH®
1/2 cup PARMESAN CHEESE
3 HARD-BOILED EGGS, grated
3/4 cup BACON BITS

In a 12 x 9 dish, layer lettuce, celery, onions, water chestnuts, peas and Monterey Jack cheese in order given. Spread mayonnaise over top, then sprinkle with sugar, Crazy Salt, Parmesan cheese, eggs and bacon bits. Cover and refrigerate for 24 hours before serving.

Pickle Salad

"A lot of cucumbers are grown in Indiana. We have a processing plant nearby that makes pickles for large grocery store chains."

Martha Molebash—Elkhart

1/2 cup VINEGAR
1 1/4 cups SUGAR
1 Tbsp. WHOLE CLOVES
2 pkgs. (1 oz. ea.) KNOX® GELATIN
1 cup COLD WATER
3 cups BOILING WATER
1 cup thinly sliced SWEET CUCUMBER
    PICKLES
1 cup thinly sliced CELERY
1 cup chopped NUTS
2-3 drops GREEN FOOD COLORING
Dash of SALT

In a large saucepan, combine vinegar, sugar and cloves; boil until thickened. In a medium mixing bowl, dissolve gelatin in cold water, add boiling water and stir. Combine the vinegar mixture with the gelatin mixture and allow to stand until it begins to settle. Stir in pickles, celery and nuts; add food coloring and salt. Pour into gelatin mold or serving bowl and refrigerate until firm.

Celery Seed Dressing

"This recipe came from my grandmother and is an old family favorite. She was a cook and housemother for Sigma Tau Gamma Fraternity at Ball State University."

Lea Ann Baker—Chesterfield

3 cups SUGAR
1 Tbsp. PAPRIKA
1 Tbsp. SALT
1 Tbsp. CELERY SEED
1 Tbsp. minced ONION
1 cup KETCHUP
1 cup VINEGAR
3 cups SALAD OIL

In a bowl, combine the first six ingredients. Slowly blend in the vinegar and oil. Serve over salad greens.

Broccoli-Cauliflower Salad

"This recipe is a special favorite at family reunions and holiday dinners."

Ruth A. Jones—Spencer

12 slices BACON
1 bunch BROCCOLI
1 head CAULIFLOWER
1 cup RAISINS

Dressing:
  1 cup MIRACLE WHIP®
  2 Tbsp. VINEGAR
  1/2 cup SUGAR

1 cup SUNFLOWER SEEDS
1/2 sm. ONION, diced
PARMESAN CHEESE

Cook, drain and crumble bacon. Cut broccoli and cauliflower into small flowerets, discarding stems. In a large bowl, combine bacon, vegetables, and all remaining ingredients (except Parmesan cheese). In a small bowl, mix dressing ingredients until smooth. Pour dressing over vegetable mixture; toss lightly to coat. Sprinkle with Parmesan cheese before serving.

Did You Know?

The country's first automatic traffic signal is believed to have been manufactured and installed in Carmel.

Sauerkraut Salad

"This is a good old German recipe that has been handed down in our family."

Charles Hauenschild—Edinburgh

1 jar (16 oz.) SAUERKRAUT
1 GREEN ONION, finely diced
1/2 GREEN BELL PEPPER,
  finely diced
1/2 RED BELL PEPPER,
  finely diced

1 stalk CELERY, finely diced
1 CARROT, shredded
1/4 cup VINEGAR
1/2 cup SUGAR
1/2 tsp. SALT
1/2 tsp. PEPPER

Drain 1/2 of the juice from the sauerkraut and discard. In a medium mixing bowl, combine all ingredients and mix well. Refrigerate for 2 days, stirring well once each day.

Cranberry Jell-O Salad

"This attractive pink Jell-O salad is a traditional Easter salad for our family. It adds a splash of spring color to the dining table and is a tasty addition to any meal."

Tara Tippett—Greenwood

1 1/2 lbs. uncooked CRANBERRIES, ground
1 can (8 oz.) crushed PINEAPPLE, well-drained
1 ORANGE, peeled, seeded and diced very small
3 cups SUGAR
3 pkgs. (3 oz. ea.) CRANBERRY JELL-O®
1 1/2 cups thinly sliced CELERY
1 cup chopped PECANS

In a large bowl, combine fruits and sugar. Add dry Jell-O to fruit mixture and stir well. Stir in celery and pecans. Refrigerate at least 24 hours before serving.

Bedford

Limestone from the Bedford area was used in constructing many notable buildings, including the Empire State Building in New York.

German Potato Salad

Nancye Barnhart—Brown County Pioneer Museum, Nashville

5 lbs. POTATOES, unpeeled
1 med. ONION, finely chopped
8 HARD-BOILED EGGS, chopped
1/2 lb. BACON
3 Tbsp. FLOUR

2 tsp. SALT
1 rounded cup SUGAR
3/4 cup CIDER VINEGAR
1/4 cup WATER

In a large Dutch oven, boil potatoes until tender; drain. Peel and slice potatoes into a bowl; toss with onion and eggs. In a skillet, fry bacon until crisp; remove from skillet, reserving drippings, drain and crumble. In a bowl, combine flour, salt and sugar, then stir in vinegar and water. Heat 8 tablespoons of bacon drippings in skillet; add flour mixture. Cook and stir until thick. Pour hot dressing over potato mixture and toss thoroughly. Sprinkle crumbled bacon over top. Serve hot.

Apple Salad & Tofu-Honey Cinnamon Dressing

Indiana Soybean Board—Lebanon

1/4 cup fresh LEMON JUICE
1 cup WATER
2 GRANNY SMITH APPLES, sliced
2 GALA APPLES, sliced
3 stalks CELERY, sliced diagonally
1 can (8 oz.) PINEAPPLE CHUNKS, drained
1/3 cup coarsely chopped WALNUTS
FRESH GREENS
MINT SPRIGS

In a bowl, combine lemon juice and water. Add sliced apples and additional water, if needed, to cover. When ready to serve, drain liquid from apples then add and combine the celery, pineapple and nuts. Add *Tofu-Honey Cinnamon Dressing* and toss gently. Serve on a bed of fresh greens; garnish with mint sprigs.

Serves 8.

Tofu-Honey Cinnamon Dressing

1 cup plain low-fat YOGURT   1 Tbsp. HONEY
1/2 cup silken TOFU   1 tsp. CINNAMON

Combine all ingredients in food processor and blend until smooth. Cover and chill.

South Bend

Founded in 1842, the University of Notre Dame is the home of the "Fighting Irish" football team. Well-known football coach Knute Rockne and the Four Horsemen of Notre Dame brought fame to this campus in the 1920s. Characterized by the distinctive golden dome of the main building, this is one of the state's most visited sites.

Main Dishes

Indiana Leg of Lamb

Indiana Sheep Breeders Association—Noblesville

Marinade:

1 cup WINE VINEGAR	2 tsp. SALT
1 cup VEGETABLE OIL	1 tsp. ROSEMARY
2 cloves GARLIC, whole	1 tsp. SAGE
1 BAY LEAF, crumbled	1/2 tsp. PEPPER

1 (5-7 lb.) boned, rolled and tied LEG OF LAMB

3 lg. POTATOES, quartered	3 lg. CHILE PEPPERS, sliced
3 lg. ONIONS, quartered	6 cloves GARLIC

Combine marinade ingredients. Place lamb in a deep glass or ceramic casserole dish; pour marinade over lamb. Cover and marinate in refrigerator for 12-24 hours, turning often. Remove lamb, strain marinade and reserve liquid. Place potatoes, onions, chiles and garlic in a shallow roasting pan; pour 1/4 cup of marinade over all. Place lamb on roasting rack over vegetables. Pour 1/4 cup marinade over lamb. Roast at 325° approximately 25 minutes per pound, or until meat thermometer registers 140° (rare) or 150° (medium). Baste with 1/4 cup marinade every 20-30 minutes. Allow lamb to rest 15 minutes before carving. Serve with vegetables. Make gravy from drippings if desired.

Mini-Hog Roast with Gravy

"Our mini-hog roast has received many awards throughout Indiana!" (see front cover photo)

Cindy Shoup Cacy—Shoup's Country Foods, Inc., Frankfort

1 (4-6 lb.) SHOUP'S MINI-HOG ROAST®
3 cups WATER

Gravy:

3 Tbsp. CORNSTARCH	2 cups BROTH from roast
1 cup COLD WATER	1 tsp. SHOUP'S® SEASONING
1/4 tsp. PEPPER	1 tsp. LEMON JUICE
1 tsp. WORCESTERSHIRE SAUCE	1 sm. can (2.5 oz.) SLICED MUSHROOMS

Thaw roast in refrigerator for one day before cooking. Place in roasting pan, add water and cook at 325° for 2-3 hours. Check roast periodically with meat thermometer until roast reaches 155° internally. Remove roast from pan; strain drippings, reserving 2 cups broth. Allow roast to set for 20 minutes before slicing. To make gravy, dissolve cornstarch in water and pour into roasting pan. Add remaining ingredients except mushrooms and bring to a boil stirring constantly until clear and thickened. Add mushrooms. Pour gravy over roast and serve.

Serves 10-12.

Cheese & Ham Casserole

1 pkg. (8 oz.) MACARONI	2 cups diced cooked HAM
1/2 cup diced ONION	2 cups grated CHEDDAR CHEESE, divided
1/4 cup BUTTER	1 cup soft BREAD CRUMBS
1 can (16 oz.) STEWED TOMATOES	

In a saucepan, cook macaroni according to package directions. Cook onion in water with macaroni. Drain. Add butter, tomatoes, ham and 1 cup of cheese; mix well. Place mixture in a greased 13 x 9 casserole dish and top with remaining cheese. Sprinkle bread crumbs evenly over top. Bake for 30 minutes in a 350° oven.

Holiday Pork Loin

"We serve this special dish every Christmas at our cafe. It's a great old-fashioned Christmas favorite."

John Pappas—B & J's American Cafe, LaPorte

1 (5 lb.) PORK LOIN ROAST
1 cup sliced ONION
1 1/2 cups sliced CARROTS

1 cup chopped GREEN BELL
  PEPPER
1/4 cup OLIVE OIL

Spice Mixture:
  2 tsp. SALT
  2 tsp. ROSEMARY LEAVES
  1 1/2 tsp. OREGANO LEAVES
  1 1/2 tsp. THYME LEAVES

  1 1/2 tsp. SAGE
  1/4 tsp. PEPPER
  1/4 tsp. NUTMEG

Gravy:
  2 cups HOT WATER
  1/4 cup FLOUR

  1/4 cup WATER
  SALT and PEPPER

Preheat oven to 350°. Place roast in a shallow pan and scatter onion, carrots and bell pepper around it. Drizzle top with olive oil then sprinkle with the spice mixture. Cover with plastic wrap and cover again with aluminum foil, sealing tightly. Roast for 3 hours or until thermometer temperature reaches 185°. Remove roast and vegetables to a serving platter. To make gravy: Strain roasting pan drippings and return them to roasting pan. Add hot water and stir well to combine. In a small bowl, combine flour and water; stir to a smooth consistency. Bring drippings to a boil and then whisk in flour mixture, stirring constantly. Cook to desired thickness. Add salt and pepper to taste. Pour gravy into a serving dish and serve with roast and vegetables.

Did You Know?

The Nappanee agricultural region in north central Indiana is known for its onion and mint crops.

Baked Salmon with Cheese Sauce

"My wife invented this recipe when I began fishing regularly on Lake Michigan and we felt we needed a new recipe."

Capt. Mike Schoonveld—Brother Nature Fishing Adventures,
Morocco

Cheese Sauce:
3 Tbsp. BUTTER
3 Tbsp. FLOUR
1 1/2 cups LIGHT CREAM

1 cup grated CHEDDAR CHEESE
1/2 tsp. SALT

6 COHO FILLETS or CHINOOK STEAKS
1/2 cup grated ONION
1 Tbsp. LEMON JUICE
SALT and PEPPER
1/4 cup melted BUTTER

In a skillet, melt butter, add flour and stir mixture until smooth. Gradually add cream, stirring until mixture boils. Cook over low heat for 6 minutes. Add cheese and salt and continue to cook until cheese melts. Remove skillet from heat. Place salmon in a buttered baking dish. Sprinkle with onion, lemon juice and season with salt and pepper to taste. Pour melted butter over top. Bake in a 400° oven for 35 minutes. Remove from oven, pour cheese sauce over the salmon and brown under broiler.

Indiana Pork Chops

"This is a delicious Indiana-style meal!"

Karen Evans Tislow—Battle Ground

6 PORK CHOPS, salted
1 1/2 cups packed BROWN SUGAR
3 Tbsp. VINEGAR

1 tsp. MUSTARD
Pinch of GINGER

Arrange pork chops in a 13 x 9 baking pan. In a small bowl, combine remaining ingredients, mix well and spread over pork chops. Cover and bake at 350° for 1 1/2 hours.

Amish Bread Stuffing

"My mother is of Amish heritage; this is one of her recipes."

Rosannah E. Shaw—Elkhart

1 lb. loaf BREAD, torn into
    bite-size pieces
2 cups cooked and deboned
    CHICKEN
2 EGGS
1 CARROT, grated
1 POTATO, grated
1 ONION, chopped

1 Tbsp. CELERY FLAKES
1/4 tsp. SAGE
1 tsp. PARSLEY
1/4 tsp. THYME
1 tsp. SALT
1/4 tsp. PEPPER
1 1/2 cups CHICKEN BROTH
1/2 cup MARGARINE

In a large mixing bowl, combine all ingredients and mix thoroughly. Place in a greased 2-quart casserole dish. Bake at 350° for 1 1/2 hours.

Elkhart
Manufacturers in this city produce more than 50 percent of our nation's band instruments.

Haystack Dinner

"Something for everyone! We were first served this tasty dish by friends soon after we moved to Indiana. It is a popular recipe that we now often serve to our friends when they come to dinner."

Aaron and Mary Jane Hoober—Trolley Cafe, Goshen

CRACKER CRUMBS
Cooked RICE

GROUND BEEF, cooked
TACO SEASONING

Choice of Condiments:
    Chopped LETTUCE
    Chopped TOMATOES
    Diced GREEN BELL PEPPER
    Sliced CELERY
    Diced CARROTS
    BLACK or GREEN OLIVES
    Chopped ONION

RAISINS
NUTS
SUNFLOWER SEEDS
SALSA
CHEESE SAUCE
Shredded CHEDDAR CHEESE

Layer in order, cracker crumbs, rice and ground beef on a plate. Add taco seasoning to taste. Select your favorite toppings and layer in any order to build your own "haystack."

Midwest Swiss Steak & Tomato Gravy

"This is my mother Naomi Walter's recipe (I added the mushrooms). My brothers always asked for this for Sunday dinner."

Barb Fausett—Frankfort

3/4 cup FLOUR
3 tsp. SALT
3/4 tsp. PEPPER
3 lbs. CHUCK STEAK, cut
   1 to 2-inches thick
4 Tbsp. OLIVE OIL, divided
3 med. ONIONS, sliced

3 cans (10.75 oz. ea.) TOMATO
   SOUP
1 can WATER
2 cans (4 oz. ea.) MUSHROOM
   STEMS and PIECES,
   drained

In a small bowl, mix flour, salt and pepper. Coat steak with flour mixture and, using a meat tenderizer, pound flour into the meat. In a heavy skillet, heat 2 tablespoons of oil and brown steaks very slowly. In a small skillet, heat 2 tablespoons of oil and sauté onions until translucent; drain. Place steak in a baking dish. Combine onions, soup, water and mushrooms and stir. Pour over steak and cover. Bake at 350° for 2 hours or until meat is tender, skimming excess grease from surface.

Serves 8-10.

Indiana Dunes National Lakeshore

The Indiana Dunes National Lakeshore, a 15,000 acre National Park, is located on Lake Michigan's south shore in northwest Indiana. Mt. Baldy, the largest "live" dune here, is 123 feet tall and is moving away from the lake at a rate of four to five feet each year. The northwest winds that move the dunes, blow sand off the top of Mt. Baldy creating the effect of a "smoking dune." Dune ridges farthest from the lake are the oldest and mark former shores of a once larger Lake Michigan.

Beefy Tofu Enchiladas

This recipe is from Indiana's 40,000 soybean farmers, who
urge you to include more soy in your diet.

Indiana Soybean Board—Lebanon

1/2 cup chopped ONION
1 lb. GROUND BEEF, browned and drained
1 can (4 oz.) chopped GREEN CHILES, drained
1 clove GARLIC, minced
1 tsp. dried CILANTRO
1 pkg. (10.5 oz.) firm TOFU, mashed
1/2 tsp. CUMIN SEED
2 cups diced TOMATO, drained
8 (8-inch) FLOUR TORTILLAS
2 cups thick TOMATO SALSA
1 cup shredded CHEDDAR CHEESE

Preheat oven to 350°. Lightly spray a 13 x 9 baking dish
with non-stick spray. In a bowl, combine all ingredients except
tortillas, salsa and cheese. Place 1/2 cup of mixture in center of
each tortilla and roll. Place rolls in a baking dish, seam side
down. Pour salsa over top and sprinkle with shredded cheese.
Cover pan with aluminum foil and bake for 25-30 minutes.

Hoosier Chicken Pot Pie

"My family's favorite dish for lunch or dinner."

Kelly Constantino—Indianapolis

1 CHICKEN, boiled until tender
2 stalks CELERY, diced
2 CARROTS, peeled and diced
4 med. POTATOES, peeled
    and cubed
1 ONION, chopped
1 can (10.75 oz.) CREAM
    OF CHICKEN SOUP
SALT and PEPPER
2 (9-inch) unbaked PIE
    CRUSTS

Remove meat from chicken bones and dice. Boil celery,
carrots, potatoes and onion until slightly tender. Drain vegetables and then stir in chicken and soup. Add salt and pepper
to taste. Place pie crust in pie pan and fill with chicken mixture.
Add top crust; seal edges and prick top with a fork. Bake at 350°
for 25-30 minutes, or until top is golden brown.

Pork Steaks
with Sour Cream Salsa

"Indiana produces a lot of pork so I've taken an Indiana ingredient and created a recipe that also reflects the years I lived in California."

Lea Ann Baker—Chesterfield

Pork Rub:
   1 Tbsp. CHILI POWDER
   1/4 tsp. CUMIN
   1 Tbsp. RED WINE VINEGAR

4 PORK STEAKS

   In a small bowl, mix chili powder, cumin and wine vinegar, then rub into steaks. Broil to desired level of doneness and serve with ***Sour Cream Salsa*** on the side.

Sour Cream Salsa

2 TOMATOES, chopped
1/2 cup chopped ONION
1 can (4 oz.) chopped GREEN
   CHILES, drained
1 bunch fresh CILANTRO, chopped
1 tsp. SALT
1 tsp. chopped GARLIC

Dash of OIL
Dash of RED WINE VINEGAR
BLACK PEPPER
CUMIN
RED PEPPER FLAKES
1 ctn. (8 oz.) SOUR CREAM,
   room temperature

   In a bowl, combine all ingredients except sour cream. Add sour cream to vegetable mixture to taste.

Wyandotte

Big Wyandotte Cave, located in southern Indiana, is one of the largest caverns in the state. This attraction features extensive rooms, over 10 miles of underground passageways and rare helictites (unusual forms of stalactites) that are said to be the largest of their type in the world.

Old-Fashioned Chicken & Dumplings

"This is an old farm recipe handed down from my great-grandmother, Grandma Brian."

Betty J. Richardson—Lebanon

1 (4-5 lb.) STEWING CHICKEN,   **1 cup FLOUR**
   cut into pieces   **1 tsp. SALT**

Sprinkle chicken with salt and place in a large kettle filled with enough water to cover. Bring to a boil, reduce heat, cover and simmer for 1 hour or until meat is tender. Remove chicken from kettle and set aside. In a small mixing bowl, combine flour, salt and enough chicken broth to make a firm dough. Turn dough out onto a heavily floured surface and sprinkle top with flour. Roll out dough with a floured rolling pin until thin like pie crust. Cut into 1 to 2-inch slices. Heat broth to a simmer and carefully drop in dumplings. Cook, covered, for 15-20 minutes.

Fort Wayne

This city was named for the Revolutionary War figure, General "Mad" Anthony Wayne after he made peace with the original inhabitants of the area, the Miami Indians.

Baked Ham

"This recipe comes from my first husband, William Bredemeyer, and our business Bredemeyer's Lunch and Waynewood Inn."

Patricia L. Green—Fort Wayne

1 (20-25 lb.) HAM
PREPARED MUSTARD
WHOLE CLOVES
3/4 cup SUGAR
1 1/4 cups WHITE PORT WINE or 1 can (12 oz.) BEER

Score ham, cover with mustard and insert cloves in each cross of scoring. Cover with sugar. Pour wine or beer over ham. Bake at 300° for 5-6 hours.

Aunt Fran's Smothered Chicken Brazilian

"My son requested this 'chicken with the green stuff on it' for his 30th birthday dinner! This recipe is from Aunt Frances Carr."

Carol J. Carr—Edinburgh

2 slices BACON	2 tsp. BOUQUET GARNI®
6 LEMON SLICES	FLAKES
1/2 cup WATER	1/4 tsp. PEPPER
2 CARROTS	1/4 tsp. powdered BAY LEAF
2 ONIONS, quartered	1 (3-4 lb.) CHICKEN, sectioned
2 Tbsp. PARSLEY FLAKES	2 cups BEEF or CHICKEN
1 tsp. SALT	BOUILLON

Garnish:
 Minced PARSLEY
 Cooked GREEN PEAS or diced HARD-BOILED EGGS

Cut bacon into squares and arrange half in the bottom of a deep frying pan. Layer with lemon slices, then add remaining bacon and water. Place carrots, onions and seasonings on top, then arrange chicken pieces over all. Pour bouillon over chicken. Cover and simmer for 2 hours or until chicken is tender. Garnish chicken with parsley and peas or diced eggs.

Fountain City

Fugitive slaves seeking freedom in Canada passed through Fountain City, a Quaker community that served as a station of the underground railroad. Leaders of the effort, Levi and Catharine Coffin opened their home to more than 2,000 fleeing slaves, none of whom was ever captured. The Coffins were the Quakers after whom the characters of Simeon and Rachel Halliday of "Uncle Tom's Cabin" were patterned.

Roast Pork & Kraut

"Indiana has many hog farms and pork is readily available. 'Pork and Kraut' is served in many of the German restaurants of central Indiana and at every Oktoberfest."

Hildegard Green—Greenwood

1 (3-4 lb.) PORK ROAST	1 lg. ONION, thinly sliced
SALT and PEPPER	1 APPLE, cored, quartered
1 jar (32 oz.) SAUERKRAUT	and sliced
1/2 sm. head CABBAGE,	1 tsp. CARAWAY SEED
thinly sliced	1 cup WATER

Sprinkle roast with salt and pepper to taste. Place roast in crockpot and alternate layers of sauerkraut, cabbage, onion and apple over top. Add caraway seed to water and pour over all. Cover and cook on low for 6-8 hours, or high for 4-5 hours, stirring several times during the cooking time.

Did You Know?

Indianapolis entrepreneur, Madam C. J. Walker, who created best-selling beauty products, was one of this country's first female African-American millionaires.

German Skillet Meal

"My family has always loved this dish."

Helen Phillips—Greensburg

1 lb. GROUND BEEF	1 cup RICE
2 Tbsp. BUTTER or	2 cans (8 oz. ea.) TOMATO SAUCE
MARGARINE	1 can (16 oz.) SAUERKRAUT,
1 cup chopped ONION	drained
1 1/4 tsp. SALT	1/2 tsp. CARAWAY SEED, optional
1/2 tsp. PEPPER	1 cup WATER

In a large skillet, sauté beef in butter until it begins to brown. Add onion, salt and pepper and continue to sauté until beef is well-browned. Stir in rice, tomato sauce, sauerkraut, caraway seed and water; bring to a boil. Reduce heat, cover and simmer for 25 minutes or until rice is tender.

Currant Glazed Duckling with Apple-Walnut Stuffing

"This is our all-time favorite duckling recipe."

Vickey Brooks—Maple Leaf Farms, Milford

1 (4-5 lb.) frozen MAPLE LEAF FARMS® DUCKLING, thawed
1/2 tsp. SALT

Currant Glaze:
    1 jar (10 oz.) CURRANT JELLY
    1/4 cup RED WINE VINEGAR
    4 WHOLE CLOVES
    1 (3-inch) stick CINNAMON

Wash and drain duckling; dry skin gently with paper towel. Sprinkle body and neck cavities with salt. Fill neck and body cavities loosely with *Apple-Walnut Stuffing.* Skewer neck skin to back. Cover opening of body with aluminum foil and tie legs together loosely. Place on rack in shallow roasting pan. Bake at 325° until drumstick meat is tender, for approximately 3 hours. To make glaze, combine jelly, vinegar and spices in a saucepan. Place over low heat and bring to a boil; simmer gently for 3 minutes. Brush duckling with glaze several times during last 30 minutes of baking time. Serve duckling with remaining glaze sauce.

Serves 4.

Apple-Walnut Stuffing

1 1/2 cups diced or thinly sliced CELERY
1/4 cup BUTTER or MARGARINE
2 cups peeled and chopped APPLES
2 cups (1/2-inch) BREAD CUBES
1/2 cup WALNUTS, chopped
2 Tbsp. BROWN SUGAR
1/4 tsp. SALT

In a skillet, sauté celery in butter until tender but not brown. Add apples, bread cubes, walnuts, brown sugar and salt; toss gently to mix.

Salmon Loaf
with Piquant Sauce

Capt. Mike Schoonveld—Brother Nature Fishing Adventures,
Morocco

1/4 cup chopped ONION
1 lb. cooked and flaked SALMON
2 cups soft BREAD CRUMBS
1/2 tsp. LAWRY'S® SEASONED SALT
1 EGG, lightly beaten

In a skillet, sauté onion, then combine in a large bowl with remaining ingredients. Shape salmon mixture into a loaf on a greased shallow baking pan. Bake at 350° for 35-40 minutes. When serving, spoon *Piquant Sauce* over top.

Piquant Sauce

2 Tbsp. chopped ONION
5 Tbsp. BUTTER
2 Tbsp. FLOUR
1 tsp. MUSTARD

SALT and PEPPER
1 1/4 cup MILK
1 tsp. WORCESTERSHIRE
SAUCE

In a skillet, sauté onion in butter until tender. Blend in flour, mustard and salt and pepper to taste. Add milk and Worcestershire sauce. Cook, stirring constantly, until sauce bubbles and thickens.

Bass Bake

4-6 BASS FILLETS
1/2 cup CORNMEAL
1 Tbsp. FLOUR
SALT and PEPPER

1/4 tsp. OLD BAY® SEASONING
4-6 slices BACON
1 med. ONION, thinly sliced

Wash and drain bass fillets. Combine cornmeal, flour, salt, pepper and seasoning in a shallow bowl. Dredge bass in cornmeal mixture. Place bass in one layer in a greased baking dish and top with bacon slices. Place onion around bass. Bake for 20 minutes at 425° or until fish flakes easily with a fork.

Glazed Country Ribs

"I prefer meaty country ribs for grilling. To ensure tenderness (and quick cooking on the grill), I precook the ribs."

Annie Watts—Roachdale

6-8 lbs. country-style PORK RIBS	2 tsp. THYME leaves
1 BAY LEAF	SALT and PEPPERCORNS
1 large ONION, quartered	

In a large kettle, place ribs, bay leaf, onion, thyme and season with salt and peppercorns; cover with water. Bring to a boil. Reduce heat; cover and simmer for 45 minutes or until tender. Remove ribs. Cover and refrigerate until ready to grill. Trim fat from ribs; brush with **Fruit Glaze.** Coat grill rack with vegetable cooking spray. Grill ribs until heated through, turning and brushing frequently with **Fruit Glaze.**

Serves 10.

Fruit Glaze

1 cup APRICOT or PEACH PRESERVES, ORANGE MARMALADE
    or RED PLUM JELLY
1 cup BARBECUE SAUCE or KETCHUP
1/2 cup packed BROWN SUGAR
2 Tbsp. DIJON MUSTARD
2 Tbsp. LEMON JUICE
2 Tbsp. WORCESTERSHIRE SAUCE
2 tsp. GARLIC POWDER
1/4 tsp. HOT PEPPER SAUCE, optional

In a medium saucepan, combine all ingredients. Simmer for 20 minutes, stirring occasionally.

Did You Know?

Amelia Earhart joined the faculty of Purdue University in 1935 as a female career consultant. It was the financing of her Lockheed Electra airplane by Purdue that enabled Amelia to fulfill her dream of circumnavigating the globe.

Potato Sausage Casserole

"I often make this for church potluck dinners."

Helen Phillips—Greensburg

1 lb. bulk PORK SAUSAGE
1 can (10.75 oz.) CREAM OF
   MUSHROOM SOUP
3/4 cup MILK
1/2 cup chopped ONION
1/2 tsp. SALT

1/4 tsp. PEPPER
3 cups peeled and sliced
   uncooked POTATOES
2 cups shredded CHEDDAR
   CHEESE
Chopped fresh PARSLEY

In a skillet, brown sausage; drain and set aside. In a small bowl, combine soup, milk, onion, salt and pepper. In a greased 2-quart casserole dish, layer 1/2 of the potatoes, 1/2 of the soup mixture and 1/2 of the sausage. Repeat layer, ending with the sausage. Cover and bake at 350° for 1 hour or until potatoes are tender. Sprinkle top with cheese and continue baking, uncovered, 2-3 minutes more, or until cheese has melted. Garnish with parsley.

Serves 6-8.

Baked Trout Au Gratin

"My husband ran sportfishing charters on Lake Michigan for 20 years. We often gave them recipes that matched their catch!"

Rolena Yagelski—Michigan City

1 lb. TROUT FILLETS
8 slices AMERICAN CHEESE
1/4 cup chopped PARSLEY
1 tsp. OREGANO
Dash of BASIL or THYME

1 cup chopped ONION
1/4 cup CORN OIL
2 Tbsp. CORNSTARCH
SALT and PEPPER
1 1/2 cups MILK

Place trout in a lightly greased 10 x 6 baking dish; layer cheese over top. Sprinkle with parsley, oregano and basil. In a skillet, sauté onion in oil until tender. Stir in cornstarch and season with salt and pepper to taste. Remove from heat and slowly pour in milk. Bring mixture to a boil, stirring constantly for 1-2 minutes. Pour onion mixture over fish. Bake at 400° for 20-30 minutes or until fish flakes easily with a fork.

Twice-Cooked Spaghetti

"I was born and raised in Cass County and am a direct descendant of some of the earliest settlers there."

Mary E. Gifford—Lebanon

Cooked leftover SPAGHETTI
1 can (10.75 oz.) CREAM OF MUSHROOM or CREAM
   OF CHICKEN SOUP
1/4 can WATER
1 jar (2.5 oz.) sliced MUSHROOMS
1 can (10 oz.) CHUNK CHICKEN, drained
1-2 Tbsp. chopped ONION
1/8 tsp. MRS. DASH® HERB BLEND, or favorite HERBS
SALT and PEPPER
1/2 cup grated CHEESE
1/3 cup MILK

Add leftover spaghetti to a large (5 lb.) container until full, freezing between additions. When ready to use, thaw frozen spaghetti by pouring hot water over it in a strainer; do not let it stand in water. In a large bowl, combine remaining ingredients, except for cheese and milk. Add spaghetti and toss until well-mixed. Layer 1/2 of the mixture in a greased 11 x 9 baking dish, sprinkle with 1/2 of the cheese then spread with remaining spaghetti mixture. Make a small well in center of casserole and pour in milk. Sprinkle top of spaghetti with remaining cheese. Bake at 350° for 20-30 minutes.

Variations: Replace cheese and water with sliced celery and a small can of sliced water chestnuts or bean sprouts (include liquids).

Note: If freshly cooked spaghetti is used, be sure to rinse, drain and cool completely.

Jazz Legend

One of America's leading songwriters, Hoagland (Hoagy) Howard Carmichael was born in Bloomington. Among his famous songs are "Star Dust," "Lazy Bones," "Rockin' Chair" and "Georgia on My Mind."

Country Chicken

"This is a hearty and delicious chicken recipe."

Roberta F. Evans—Rochester

2 cans (10.75 oz. ea.) CREAM OF MUSHROOM SOUP
2 cups MILK
1 cup CHICKEN BROTH
1 pkg. (8 oz.) ELBOW MACARONI, uncooked
3 cups chopped cooked CHICKEN
1/3 cup grated PARMESAN CHEESE, 2 Tbsp. reserved
1 sm. ONION, minced
4 HARD-BOILED EGGS, sliced
1 tsp. GARLIC SALT
3 PIMENTOS, drained and chopped

In a 13 x 9 baking pan, blend together soup, milk and broth. Stir in macaroni, chicken, cheese (reserve 2 tablespoons), onion, eggs, garlic salt and pimentos. Bake, covered, at 350° for 1 hour and 25 minutes. Uncover, sprinkle reserved Parmesan cheese over top and bake an additional 5 minutes.

Sweet & Sour Meatloaf

"Years ago, when my children were small, I made this dish for them and it became a favorite."

Helen Phillips—Greensburg

1 1/2 lbs. GROUND BEEF
1 med. ONION, finely chopped
1 cup CRACKER CRUMBS
1/4 tsp. PEPPER
1 1/2 tsp. SALT
1/2 cup TOMATO PASTE

1 EGG, beaten
1/2 cup TOMATO SAUCE
1 cup WATER
2 Tbsp. VINEGAR
2 Tbsp. MUSTARD
2 Tbsp. BROWN SUGAR

In a medium mixing bowl, combine beef and onion and mix well. Add the next 5 ingredients to mixture. Shape into a loaf and place in a loaf pan or baking dish. In a small bowl, combine remaining ingredients and spread over the meatloaf. Bake at 350° for 1 1/2 hours, basting often with tomato sauce mixture.

Baked Spaghetti

"This is delicious served on a cold, snowy Indiana day."

Shiela DeBoer—Eenigenburg Blueberry Farm, Demotte

1 lb. GROUND BEEF
1 lg. ONION, chopped
1 GREEN BELL PEPPER, chopped
2 cans (10.75 oz. ea.) TOMATO SOUP
1 can (4 oz.) MUSHROOMS, drained
1 Tbsp. WORCESTERSHIRE SAUCE
1 pkg. (8 oz.) THIN SPAGHETTI
2 cups grated SHARP CHEDDAR CHEESE

In a skillet, brown beef, remove and set aside in a large bowl. Add onion and bell pepper to skillet and sauté until tender; drain. Combine soup, mushrooms and Worcestershire sauce with beef; stir in onion and bell pepper. Prepare spaghetti according to package directions. Place spaghetti in a buttered 13 x 9 pan and pour beef mixture over the top. Sprinkle with cheese. Bake at 350° for 35-40 minutes.

Hamburger Casserole

"This is a very easy and inexpensive way to make a delicious ground beef dish."

Frances K. Idzik—Schererville

1 med. ONION, chopped
3 Tbsp. BUTTER
1 lb. GROUND BEEF
3/4 tsp. SALT

PEPPER
7 cups chopped CABBAGE
1 can (10.75 oz.) TOMATO SOUP

In a skillet, sauté onion in butter until translucent. Add ground beef and brown lightly; add salt and pepper to taste. Place 4 cups of cabbage in a 2-quart baking dish. Cover with meat mixture and then layer with remaining cabbage. Pour soup on top of the cabbage. Bake, covered, at 350° for 1 hour.

Note: Do not add any water to recipe, it makes its own juices.

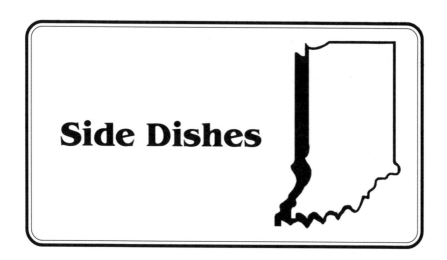

Curry Lima Bean Casserole

"Indiana has many gardens full of lima beans. I wanted to use them in a different way, with a new taste, so I created this recipe."

Mildred Chambers—Muncie

2 1/2 cups BABY LIMA BEANS
2 med. ONIONS, chopped
1 RED or GREEN BELL PEPPER, sliced
1 can (10.75 oz.) CREAM OF MUSHROOM SOUP
1/2 cup WATER (reserved from cooked beans)
1 cup SOUR CREAM
1 1/2 tsp. CURRY POWDER
1/4 cup seasoned BREAD CRUMBS
1 Tbsp. BUTTER, melted
2 slices BACON, cooked and crumbled

In a saucepan, cook lima beans until tender; drain, reserving 1/2 cup of cooking liquid. Place beans in a large bowl. In a saucepan, combine onion, bell pepper, soup and water and heat thoroughly. Remove from heat and blend in sour cream and curry powder. Pour mixture over the beans and stir well. Spoon into a 2-quart casserole dish. Combine bread crumbs with butter, stir in bacon and sprinkle mixture over the beans. Bake, uncovered, at 350° for 25 minutes until top is golden brown.

Serves 4.

Huber Farm's Scalloped Mushroom Potatoes

"This was my mother's recipe."

Beverly Huber Engleman—Joe Huber Family Farm & Restaurant, Starlight

1 can (10.75 oz.) MUSHROOM SOUP
2/3 cup MILK
2 Tbsp. chopped PIMENTO
1 can (4 oz.) MUSHROOM STEMS & PIECES, drained
3/4 cup grated CHEDDAR CHEESE, divided
SALT and PEPPER
4 cups thinly sliced, uncooked POTATOES

In a large bowl, combine soup and milk and mix until well-blended. Stir in pimento, mushrooms, 1/2 cup of cheese, salt and pepper to taste. Add potatoes and mix well. Pour mixture into a lightly greased 2-quart casserole dish and top with remaining cheese. Bake at 375° for 1 1/2 hours.

Parke County

Parke County is known as "The Covered Bridge Capital of the World" with more than 30 covered bridges. The 207-foot bridge over Sugar Creek is the longest single-span covered bridge in the country.

Corn Pudding

"This recipe has been shared by many over the years."

Viola Ayers Collins—Lebanon

4 Tbsp. FLOUR
4 Tbsp. SUGAR
2 tsp. SALT
2 sticks MARGARINE or BUTTER, melted

4 EGGS, beaten
1 1/2 cups MILK
1/4 cup chopped ONION
2 cans (15 oz. ea.) WHITE CREAM STYLE CORN

In a large bowl, combine flour, sugar and salt and mix well. Add butter, eggs and milk and blend. Stir in onion and corn; mix well. Pour into a greased 13 x 9 pan. Bake at 350° for 1 hour.

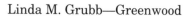

Baked Carrots

"This was my great-grandmother's recipe; she was a full-blooded Cherokee Indian. She always said that carrots from her garden and eggs from her chickens came in handy if the corn crop dried up. We serve these carrots at all of our holiday dinners."

Linda M. Grubb—Greenwood

1 lb. CARROTS, peeled
2 EGGS
1 1/2 cups CRACKERS, crushed
1 stick MARGARINE, melted

Cut carrots in half, then slice lengthwise to make "wedges." In a medium saucepan, cook carrots in water until just tender; drain and allow to cool. In a pie pan, beat eggs. Dip carrot wedges into the eggs then roll in cracker crumbs. Pour 1/2 of the margarine onto a cookie sheet, arrange carrots on sheet, then pour remaining margarine over the top. Bake carrots at 400° for 35-40 minutes or until crisp.

Indiana Invents Pork & Beans!

Gilbert Van Camp, an Indiana grocer, used his wife's recipe to help sustain Union troops during the civil war by providing them with his invention of canned pork and beans.

Barbecued Baked Beans

Cindy Shoup Cacy—Shoup's Country Foods, Inc., Frankfort

2 cans (16 oz. ea.) PORK & BEANS
1 sm. ONION, diced
1 cup packed BROWN SUGAR
2 Tbsp. YELLOW MUSTARD
1 jar (19 oz.) SHOUP'S® BARBECUE SAUCE
6 strips BACON, cut into squares
SHOUP'S® SEASONING, to taste

Combine all ingredients and place in a casserole dish. Bake for 1 hour at 350°.

Serves 8-10.

Grandmother's Cabbage Casserole

"This is a very old and very good recipe."

Christine Litsey—Elwood

1 med. head CABBAGE
4 Tbsp. BUTTER
4 Tbsp. FLOUR
1/2 tsp. SALT
1/2 tsp. PEPPER
2 cups MILK

Topping:
  1/2 GREEN BELL PEPPER, chopped
  1/2 RED BELL PEPPER, chopped
  1/2 ONION, chopped
  1/2 cup MAYONNAISE
  3 Tbsp. CHILI SAUCE
  1 1/2 cups shredded CHEDDAR CHEESE, divided
  GARLIC BREAD CRUMBS

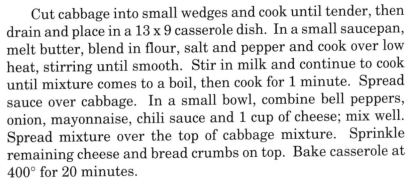

Cut cabbage into small wedges and cook until tender, then drain and place in a 13 x 9 casserole dish. In a small saucepan, melt butter, blend in flour, salt and pepper and cook over low heat, stirring until smooth. Stir in milk and continue to cook until mixture comes to a boil, then cook for 1 minute. Spread sauce over cabbage. In a small bowl, combine bell peppers, onion, mayonnaise, chili sauce and 1 cup of cheese; mix well. Spread mixture over the top of cabbage mixture. Sprinkle remaining cheese and bread crumbs on top. Bake casserole at 400° for 20 minutes.

Serves 10-12.

Long Beach

Local legend describes this area as a popular hideout of the 1920s Chicago gangsters such as Al Capone and Bugsy Malone.

Grandma Lukaczyk's Pierogi

"My maternal grandparents came from the Ukraine. We had pierogi for Christmas Eve and Easter feasts."

Paula Teibel—Hammond

Potato Filling (prepare ahead and chill):
- 5 lbs. RED POTATOES, peeled and chopped
- 1 lb. BUTTER, divided
- 1 ONION, minced
- 1 lb. AMERICAN CHEESE, diced

Dough:
- 5 cups FLOUR
- 2 cups WARM WATER
- 1/8 cup BUTTER, melted
- 2 EGGS, beaten

In a large pot, boil potatoes in unsalted water; drain and set aside. In a medium skillet, melt 1 stick of butter; add onion and sauté until translucent. Add potatoes, remaining butter and cook until tender; drain well. In a large bowl, combine onion, potatoes and cheese. Cover and allow to sit until cheese starts to melt, then mash with potato masher until well-blended. Cover and place in refrigerator for 12-24 hours. In a medium mixing bowl, combine ingredients for dough and mix well. If dough is too sticky, add more flour a little at a time to handling consistency. Divide the dough into small portions and roll out until 1/8-inch thick. Cut out circles using a glass or a round cookie cutter. Place a rounded tablespoon of potato filling on each dough circle; fold and seal edges with a fork. Drop carefully into boiling water and cook until they rise to the top; remove with a slotted spoon.

Yields 6 dozen.

Wabash

Wabash became the first city in the world to be illuminated by electricity when the courthouse dome lit up on March 31, 1880.

Cabbage & Tomatoes

"This recipe was a favorite of the wife of our former Indiana Governor, Otis Bowen."

Hildegard Green—Greenwood

1/2 cup chopped ONION
4 Tbsp. BUTTER or
    MARGARINE
3 Tbsp. FLOUR
2 cups TOMATOES
2 tsp. WORCESTERSHIRE
    SAUCE

1/2 tsp. SUGAR
3/4 tsp. SALT
1/4 tsp. PEPPER
3 slices BREAD, cubed
6 cups shredded CABBAGE
1/4 lb. AMERICAN
    CHEESE, cubed

In a medium skillet, sauté onion in 3 tablespoons of butter until translucent. Blend in flour until smooth, then add tomatoes, Worcestershire sauce, sugar, salt and pepper. In a separate skillet, lightly brown bread cubes in remaining butter. Cook cabbage in boiling water for 5 minutes; drain. In a 2-quart casserole dish, layer 1/2 of the cabbage, top with 1/2 of the tomato mixture, 1/2 of the bread and 1/2 of the cheese; follow with another layer of each, ending with the cheese on top. Bake at 375° for 30 minutes.

Santa Claus

This southern Indiana city receives over 500,000 letters during the Christmas season!

Baked Sauerkraut

"This is a delicious side dish."

Roberta F. Evans—Rochester

1 qt. SAUERKRAUT, drained
1 lg. can (28 oz.) WHOLE TOMATOES, cut into pieces
1/2 lb. diced uncooked BACON
2 cups SUGAR

In a medium mixing bowl, combine all ingredients and mix well. Pour into a greased 13 x 9 baking pan. Bake at 325° for 2 hours.

Tangy Sweet 'n' Sour Tomato Sauce

"This is a great way to use Indiana's garden-fresh vegetables. This is especially good on meats or fried potatoes."

Darlene Hyndman—Fort Wayne

12 lg. TOMATOES,
    peeled and chopped
2 lg. GREEN BELL
    PEPPERS, chopped
2 lg. ONIONS, chopped

2 cloves GARLIC, diced
2 cups SUGAR
2 cups CIDER VINEGAR
2 Tbsp. SALT

In a large saucepan, combine all ingredients and simmer over low heat for 2 hours or until desired consistency. Pour into hot, sterilized jars and seal at once.

Yields 3 pints.

Hoosier Corn Casserole

"This is a delicious recipe from my husband's mother who was born and raised in Indiana. Our family enjoys it every Thanksgiving and Christmas."

Shari Altenhof—Elkhart

1 can (15.25 oz.) WHOLE KERNEL CORN
1 can (15 oz.) CREAM STYLE CORN
1 pkg. JIFFY® CORN MUFFIN MIX
2 EGGS, beaten
1/2 cup BUTTER
1 ctn. (8 oz.) SOUR CREAM
2 cups shredded SHARP CHEDDAR CHEESE

Preheat oven to 350°. Drain the whole kernel corn, reserving 1/2 of the liquid. In a large mixing bowl, combine both cans of corn, liquid from whole kernel corn, muffin mix, eggs, butter, sour cream and 2/3 of the cheese; mix well. Pour mixture into a large casserole dish. Bake, uncovered, for 30 minutes, then top with remaining cheese and bake for 10 minutes more. Allow to cool slightly before serving.

Grandma Minnie's Macaroni & Cheese

"My grandmother Minnie was born in DeKalb County. The original version of this recipe was in her 1927 Farmer's Guide Cook Book, in her own handwriting. The book is now in very bad condition but I treasure it very much. I have changed and added some of the ingredients through the years."

Glenna Brown—Auburn

1/2 lb. MACARONI, broken into small pieces
1 cup grated CHEDDAR CHEESE
1/4 cup BUTTER, softened
SALT
1 sleeve SALTINE CRACKERS, crumbled
1 cup MILK or CREAM

In a saucepan, boil macaroni in salted water for 20 minutes; drain. In a buttered pan, place a layer of the macaroni, sprinkle with 1/2 of the cheese, dot with butter and season with salt. Add another layer of macaroni, cheese and butter. Cover with cracker crumbs, then pour milk over the top. Bake at 350° for 1/2 hour or until top is brown.

Corn Casserole

"This is one of my favorite recipes."

Lena A. France—Noblesville

1 can (15.25 oz.) WHOLE KERNEL CORN
1 can (15 oz.) CREAM STYLE CORN
1 stick BUTTER, softened
1/2 cup SUGAR
1 cup SOUR CREAM
1 box JIFFY® CORN MUFFIN MIX
2 EGGS, beaten

Combine all ingredients in a large bowl and mix well. Pour into a greased 13 x 9 baking dish and bake at 350° for 1 hour.

Beet Jelly

"Co-workers gave me this recipe when I had an over-abundance of beets in my garden one year. It is delicious."

Barb Fausett—Frankfort

2 lbs. fresh BEETS, peeled	2 boxes (1.75 oz. ea.) SURE JELL®
WATER	8 cups SUGAR
1/2 cup REALEMON® CONCENTRATE	1 box (6 oz.) RED RASPBERRY JELL-O®

In a large saucepan, add beets and enough water to cover. Cook until beets are tender; drain and reserve juice and beets separately. Bring 6 cups of beet juice (adding water to reserved juice if needed), lemon concentrate and Sure Jell to a boil. Stir in sugar and Jell-O and continue to boil for 6 minutes. Pour into hot, sterilized jelly glasses or jars and seal with paraffin. Use leftover beets for a side dish.

Acorn-Cranberry Squash

"The colors, flavors and textures of this recipe are excellent!"

Caryn Davis—Indianapolis

4 sm. ACORN SQUASH

Cranberry Compote:
  1 1/2 cups whole CRANBERRIES
  1/2 cup APPLESAUCE
  1/2 tsp. grated ORANGE PEEL
  1/2 cup packed MAPLE or BROWN SUGAR
  3 tsp. COOKING OIL
  1/2 cup RAISINS
  1/2 cup WALNUTS

Preheat oven to 350°. Cut each squash in half horizontally and seed. Trim the bottom ends so that the halves will stand upright in a baking dish. Bake squash in the center of oven for about 35 minutes, or until tender. Set aside to cool. In a medium bowl, combine all compote ingredients well, then spoon into squash cavities. Return squash to oven and bake for an additional 25-30 minutes.

Hoosier Fried Corn

"This recipe came from my husband's mother, Catherine Clonics. This is his favorite way to enjoy the sweet corn from our garden."

Annie Watts—Roachdale

6 slices BACON, chopped
6 cups fresh sweet CORN KERNELS (6 to 8 ears)
1 lg. ONION, halved and sliced
1 tsp. THYME
SALT and PEPPER

In a large non-stick skillet, cook bacon until brown and crisp; remove to paper towel to drain. In bacon drippings, cook corn, onion and thyme over medium-high heat, stirring frequently until lightly browned. Season with salt and pepper. Garnish with bacon.

Serves 4.

Variations:

Smoked Sausage: Omit bacon. Slice one pound smoked link sausage and brown in 2 tablespoons of olive oil. Continue preparation as indicated.

Bell Pepper and **Zucchini:** Omit bacon. Cut 1 bell pepper into strips, and slice 1 medium-sized zucchini. Combine and sauté in 2 tablespoons of olive oil. Continue preparation as indicated.

Gary

Gary was named after Judge Elbert H. Gary, a founding member of the U. S. Steel Corporation. It was established in 1906 for steelworkers and their families. Covering almost 4,000 acres, Gary Works is now U. S. Steel's largest manufacturing plant and the largest integrated steel plant in North America.

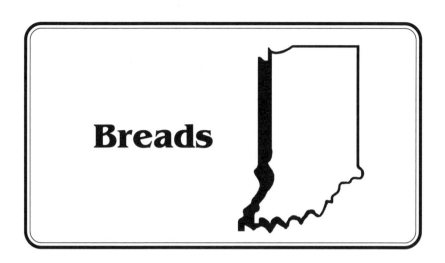

Breads

Buttermilk-Almond Scones

"These scones are always a big hit!"

Tammy Schaffer—The Washington Street Inn, Bluffton

1 EGG	1/2 cup SUGAR
1 1/2 cups BUTTERMILK	1 1/2 cups BUTTER
2 tsp. ALMOND EXTRACT	2 cups toasted ALMONDS,
4 cups FLOUR	chopped
4 tsp. BAKING POWDER	CREAM
1 tsp. BAKING SODA	SUGAR
1 tsp. SALT	Toasted ALMONDS

Preheat oven to 425°. In a bowl, beat together egg, buttermilk and almond extract. In another bowl, combine flour, baking powder, baking soda, salt and sugar. Cut in butter until mixture resembles coarse crumbs. Add almonds. Combine both mixtures and mix lightly with a fork to a soft dough. Place dough on a lightly floured surface; knead gently for 5-6 minutes. Divide dough into quarters, pat into 1/2-inch thick circles then cut each into 6 wedges. Place wedges on a greased baking sheet. Brush with cream; sprinkle with sugar and a few slices of almonds. Bake for 12-15 minutes.

Grand Champion Dill Bread

"This bread is especially good with potato soup."

Thelma Abplanalp—Greensburg

1 pkg. DRY YEAST
1/4 cup WARM WATER
2 Tbsp. SUGAR
1 cup SOUR CREAM,
    room temperature
1 EGG, beaten
1 Tbsp. BUTTER, softened

1 sm. ONION, chopped
1 Tbsp. DILL SEED
1 Tbsp. DILL WEED
1 tsp. SALT
2 3/4 cups FLOUR
1 EGG YOLK, beaten
2 tsp. WATER

In a large mixing bowl, dissolve yeast in water with sugar. Add sour cream, then stir in remaining ingredients except egg yolk and water and mix well. Turn dough out onto a lightly floured surface and knead; place in a greased bowl and let rise until doubled in bulk. Roll dough into a rectangle and cut into 3 strips. Braid strips together and pinch ends closed. Combine egg yolk and water and brush tops of strips. Cover and let rise again. Bake at 350° for 45 minutes.

Old Jail Biscuits

"The old Montgomery County jail is a circular cellblock designed to rotate 360 degrees. One day the sheriff decided to go fishing and forgot to leave the cellblock keys so that the deputies could feed the prisoners. The problem was solved by tossing the prisoners baked potatoes and biscuits through a small passway."

Tamara Hemmerlein—The Old Jail Museum, Crawfordsville

4 cups FLOUR
1 tsp. SALT
5 tsp. BAKING SODA

2/3 cup SHORTENING
1 2/3 cups MILK

In a bowl, combine flour, salt and baking soda. Cut in shortening and add milk. Mix well. Knead on a lightly floured surface. Roll out dough and cut out biscuits with a biscuit cutter. Bake at 350° for 20 minutes or until golden brown.

Crumb-Topped Blueberry Muffins

"This is a family and customer favorite!"

Wanda Bonnell—Bonnell's Blueberries, North Judson

2 1/2 cups FLOUR	1/4 cup BUTTER or
4 tsp. BAKING POWDER	MARGARINE
1/2 tsp. SALT	1 cup MILK
1/2 cup SUGAR	1 tsp. VANILLA
1 EGG	1 1/2 cups BLUEBERRIES

In a medium mixing bowl, sift together flour, baking powder and salt. In a large mixing bowl, cream together sugar, egg and butter. Add dry ingredients to creamed mixture and mix well. Stir in milk and vanilla, then fold in blueberries. Spoon batter into 12 greased large muffin cups. Sprinkle *Crumb Topping* over top of muffins. Bake at 375° for 20-25 minutes.

Crumb Topping

1/2 cup SUGAR	1/4 cup BUTTER or
1/2 tsp. CINNAMON	MARGARINE
1/3 cup FLOUR	

In a small bowl, mix all ingredients together, cutting butter into mixture until mixture is crumbly.

Terre Haute
(ter-uh-hoht)

Because of its location high on the east bank of the Wabash River, the French named this city Terre Haute, which means "high land." Clabber Girl® Baking Powder has been manufactured in downtown Terre Haute for nearly 150 years! Terre Haute is also home to the Root Glass Company which designed the original Coca-Cola® bottle.

Brown County Fried Biscuits

"A Brown County favorite! This area is very rustic and scenic with hills, woods, valleys and a State Park. This is a quaint little town at the foot of a hill where there are many shops."

Mary A. Perrault—Brownsburg

2 pkgs. DRY YEAST
1/4 cup LUKEWARM WATER
4 1/2 cups FLOUR, sifted
3 tsp. SALT
2 Tbsp. SUGAR
1/4 cup SHORTENING, melted
2 cups MILK
VEGETABLE OIL for frying

In a small bowl, sprinkle yeast in warm water and allow to dissolve; set aside. In a large mixing bowl, combine flour, salt and sugar and mix well. Stir in shortening, yeast and milk and mix until dough is smooth. Cover the bowl with a damp cloth and allow to rise until doubled in bulk. Pull off pieces of dough and roll lightly into 1 1/2-inch balls. Drop pieces into hot oil, a few at a time, and fry 2-3 minutes on each side until puffy and golden brown. Remove with a slotted spoon; drain on paper towels. Serve hot with **butter** and **apple butter.**

Richmond

The Gennett Record Company, founded in Richmond in 1915, was one of the first record labels to release early jazz music. Among the artists who recorded in Richmond were King Oliver's Creole Jazz Band (featuring Louis Armstrong's first recorded solo), Jelly Roll Morton, Duke Ellington, Hoagy Carmichael, Glen Miller and Bix Beiderbecke.

Freezer Biscuits

"Biscuits were a staple in early Indiana farm life, now we consider them a treat! These can be made ahead and frozen until needed."

Wilhelmina Burket—Lafayette

2 pkgs. DRY YEAST	1/4 cup SUGAR
1/4 cup WARM WATER	1 tsp. SALT
5 cups unsifted FLOUR	1 cup SHORTENING
4 tsp. BAKING POWDER	2 cups BUTTERMILK
1 tsp. BAKING SODA	

In a small bowl, dissolve yeast in warm water; cover to promote faster rising. Sift dry ingredients together in a large mixing bowl and then cut in shortening. Combine buttermilk with yeast, blend into flour mixture and stir until smooth. Turn dough out onto a lightly floured surface and knead 20-30 times. Roll dough out, cut into biscuits and place on baking sheet. Bake at 375° for 14 minutes. These can be enjoyed hot or frozen for later use.

Makes 24 biscuits.

Zucchini Muffins

"We serve these often to our guests."

Rosalind Slabaugh—Spring View Bed & Breakfast, Goshen

3 EGGS, beaten	1 tsp. SALT
1 cup OIL	1 tsp. BAKING POWDER
2 cups SUGAR	2 1/2 cups FLOUR
3 tsp. VANILLA	2 cups shredded ZUCCHINI
1 tsp. BAKING SODA	1 cup chopped NUTS
3 tsp. CINNAMON	

In a large mixing bowl, combine eggs, oil, sugar and vanilla and beat until smooth and creamy. Add baking soda, cinnamon, salt and baking powder and mix well. Fold in flour, zucchini and nuts. Pour batter into greased muffin tins; bake at 350° for 20 minutes.

Makes 24 muffins.

Sugarless Muffins

"I took a cake recipe and added some ingredients to make these very tasty muffins. They keep fresh for a long time and are just right for those who are diabetic."

Christine Litsey—Elwood

1 cup DATES, chopped
1 cup PRUNES, chopped
1 cup COLD WATER
1 cup RAISINS
1 stick MARGARINE, melted
1 cup FLOUR
1 tsp. BAKING SODA
1/2 tsp. SALT

2 EGGS, beaten
1 cup chopped NUTS
1/2 tsp. CINNAMON
1/2 tsp. NUTMEG
1 tsp. VANILLA
1/2 cup LOW-CALORIE, NO
   SUGAR STRAWBERRY
   SPREAD

In a saucepan, boil dates and prunes in water for 3 minutes. Stir in raisins and margarine and allow to cool. In a mixing bowl, combine flour, baking soda, salt, eggs, nuts, spices and vanilla; mix well. Add to fruit mixture, then fold in strawberry spread and stir until thoroughly mixed. Pour into greased muffin tins. Bake at 350° for 20 minutes.

Makes 12 muffins.

Blueberry-Banana Bread

"This is a favorite of our family and our customers."

Wanda Bonnell—Bonnell's Blueberries, North Judson

2 cups FLOUR
2 tsp. BAKING POWDER
1/2 tsp. SALT
1/2 tsp. BAKING SODA
3/4 cup SUGAR

1/2 cup MARGARINE
2 EGGS
3 mashed ripe BANANAS
1 cup BLUEBERRIES
1/2 cup chopped NUTS

In a large bowl, sift together flour, baking powder, salt and baking soda. In a small bowl, cream together sugar, margarine and eggs; stir in bananas. Add sifted ingredients to creamed mixture and mix well. Fold in blueberries and nuts. Pour into a greased loaf pan and bake at 350° for 1 hour.

Banana Bread

*"My sister gave me this recipe years ago.
It makes a good, moist bread."*

Marie Martin—Greensburg

1/4 cup MARGARINE	1 tsp. BAKING SODA
1 1/3 cups SUGAR	3/4 tsp. SALT
2 EGGS	1 cup SOUR CREAM
1 tsp. VANILLA	1/2 cup WALNUTS
2 cups FLOUR	1 cup mashed ripe BANANAS
1 tsp. BAKING POWDER	

In a bowl, cream margarine and sugar together, then stir in eggs and vanilla. In a large bowl, sift together dry ingredients. Add dry ingredients to creamed mixture, alternating with sour cream and stirring after each addition. Stir in nuts and bananas; mix well. Pour batter into 2 greased and floured loaf pans. Bake at 350° for 35-40 minutes.

Persimmon Bread

"We go to southern Indiana in the fall, just after a frost to pick our persimmons. We grind them up and freeze them for use all year round for this delicious bread."

Shiela DeBoer—Eenigenburg Blueberry Farm, Demotte

2 cups ground PERSIMMONS	3 1/2 cups FLOUR
4 EGGS	3 tsp. CINNAMON
1 cup OIL or 1 cup unsweetened APPLESAUCE	2 tsp. BAKING POWDER
	2 cups SUGAR
3 tsp. VANILLA	2 tsp. BAKING SODA
1/2 cup MILK	1 tsp. SALT

In a bowl, combine persimmons, eggs, oil, vanilla and milk. Mix well. Mix together dry ingredients and then add to persimmon mixture; mix well. Pour mixture into 2 greased and floured 9 x 5 loaf pans and bake at 350° for 1 hour or until toothpick inserted in center comes out clean.

Orange Blossom Buns

"I worked at our local country club for 22 years and this recipe was a top favorite there."

Thelma Abplanalp—Greensburg

5 1/2-6 1/2 cups unsifted FLOUR, divided
1 3/4 cups SUGAR, divided
1 tsp. SALT
3 pkgs. DRY YEAST
1/2 cup BUTTER or MARGARINE, softened
1 cup WARM WATER (120-130°)
3 EGGS
2 Tbsp. grated ORANGE PEEL
1/4 cup BUTTER, melted

In a large mixing bowl, combine 1 1/4 cups of flour, 3/4 cup of sugar, salt and yeast; mix thoroughly. Add butter and then gradually add water, beating at medium speed for 2 minutes and scraping the bowl occasionally. Stir in eggs and 1/4 cup of flour. Beat at high speed for 2 minutes. Stir in enough flour to make a soft dough. Turn dough out onto a lightly floured surface and knead for 8-10 minutes until smooth and elastic; let rise until doubled in bulk. Punch down, divide dough into small pieces and form into balls. In a small bowl, mix 1 cup of sugar with orange peel. Dip dough in melted butter, then in orange sugar mixture and place on baking sheet. Bake for 25-30 minutes at 350°.

Peru

In the 1800s, Peru was the home base of various traveling circuses including the well-known Hagenback-Wallace circus and was known as the "Circus Capital of America." The Circus City Festival Museum there contains many circus posters, newspaper clippings and costumes of celebrated performers.

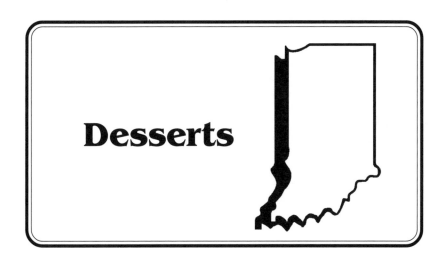

Blueberry Pizza

"Always a favorite of my family and friends. I make it ahead of time so that we can enjoy our blueberry festival without worrying about what to serve when everyone returns to the house."

Linda Rippy—Plymouth

1 (13-inch) unbaked PIE SHELL	1/2 cup SUGAR
1 pkg. (8 oz.) CREAM CHEESE	1 tsp. VANILLA
2 EGGS	1/3 cup chopped WALNUTS

Bake pie shell at 350° for 15 minutes. Blend together remaining ingredients and pour into pie crust. Return to oven for 10 minutes; cool. Pour **Blueberry Topping** over top and serve.

Blueberry Topping

4 cups BLUEBERRIES, divided	1/4 tsp. SALT
3/4 cup SUGAR, divided	1/2 cup WATER
3 Tbsp. CORNSTARCH	1 Tbsp. BUTTER
1/4 tsp. CINNAMON	

Mix 2 cups blueberries with 1/4 cup sugar; set aside. In a saucepan, mix remaining ingredients, bring to a boil and simmer until thickened. Add sugared blueberries. Cool.

Banana Oatmeal Cookies

"This is a family favorite and a great way to use up very ripe bananas. I have made these cookies for over 40 years."

Mary A. Perrault—Brownsburg

1 1/2 cups FLOUR
1 cup SUGAR
1/2 tsp. BAKING SODA
1 tsp. SALT
1/4 tsp. NUTMEG
3/4 tsp. CINNAMON
3/4 cup SHORTENING

1 EGG, well-beaten
1 cup (2-3) mashed ripe
   BANANAS
1 3/4 cups QUICK-ROLLED
   OATS
1/2 cup chopped NUTS

In a large mixing bowl, sift together flour, sugar, baking soda, salt, nutmeg and cinnamon, then cut in shortening. Add egg, bananas, oats and nuts and beat until thoroughly blended. Drop batter from a teaspoon, spaced 1 1/2-inches apart, on an ungreased cookie sheet. Bake at 400° for 15 minutes or until cookies are golden. Remove from pan immediately.

Makes 3 1/2 dozen cookies.

Great Grandma McNeil's Sugar Cookies

"This recipe has been handed down through many generations. My great grandmother and grandmother both lived in New Richmond their entire married lives."

Mavourneen McNeil Walker—Lafayette

2 cups packed LIGHT BROWN
   SUGAR
1/2 tsp. SALT
6 Tbsp. HOT WATER
1 tsp. BAKING SODA

1 cup BUTTER, softened
2 EGGS
1 tsp. VANILLA
1 1/2-2 cups FLOUR

Combine all ingredients in a large bowl, adding enough flour to make a soft dough. Roll dough out onto a lightly floured surface to 3/8-inch thick. Cut dough with cookie cutter. Place cookies on an ungreased cookie sheet and bake at 350° for 10-12 minutes.

Raspberry Truffle Brownies

"This recipe is from our own cook book, and the one most often requested by our guests."

Vickie Hunsberger—Victorian Guest House, Nappanee

Brownies:
1/2 cup MARGARINE
1 1/4 cups SEMI-SWEET CHOCOLATE CHIPS
2 EGGS
3/4 cup packed BROWN SUGAR
2 Tbsp. WATER
1/2 tsp. BAKING POWDER
3/4 cup FLOUR

Topping:
1 cup SEMI-SWEET CHOCOLATE CHIPS
1 pkg. (8 oz.) CREAM CHEESE, softened
1/4 cup POWDERED SUGAR
1/3 cup SEEDLESS RED RASPBERRY JAM

Glaze:
1/4 cup SEMI-SWEET CHOCOLATE CHIPS
1 tsp. MARGARINE

In a heavy saucepan or double boiler, melt margarine and chocolate chips over low heat. Cool slightly. In a large bowl, beat together eggs, brown sugar and water. Combine with chocolate mixture and mix well. Add baking powder and flour and stir well. Spread in a greased 9 x 9 baking pan. Bake at 350° for 30-35 minutes or until brownies test done; cool. For Topping: Place chocolate chips in a saucepan and melt over low heat; cool. In a mixing bowl, beat cream cheese until fluffy. Add powdered sugar and jam. Stir in melted chocolate and then spread over cooled brownies. For Glaze: In a saucepan, melt chocolate chips and margarine; stir. Drizzle over topping. Chill before cutting; store in refrigerator.

Greenfield

The Riley Festival is an annual celebration held in Greenfield in honor of poet laureate James Whitcomb Riley who was born here in 1849.

Red Cinnamon Apples

"After many years of just 'knowing' how to make this recipe, I finally measured all the ingredients and wrote out the recipe. These red apples have been served at family dinners for ages. Our family history has been traced back to Johnny Appleseed, who is part of Indiana's history."

Esther H. Goodwin—Noblesville

2 cups **SUGAR**
2 cups **WATER**
1/2-3/4 cup **CINNAMON RED HOT CANDIES**
Few drops **RED FOOD COLORING**
8-12 med. **JONATHAN APPLES**, peeled and cored, left whole

In a large pan, stir together sugar, water, cinnamon candies and food coloring. Bring mixture to a boil, stirring occasionally. Make sure candies and sugar are dissolved. Place apples in a single layer in the sugar mixture; add more water if needed to cover lower half of apples. Cook apples until lower half is tender, then turn apples over and continue cooking until completely tender. Using a slotted spoon, remove apples and place in a single layer in a large bowl. Continue boiling liquid gently until it falls in a sheet or stream when poured from a metal spoon. Pour sauce over apples and serve.

Potato Candy

"This recipe is from our 'Brackney Family Cookbook' which was developed by my mother and father. The book is now used as a fund-raiser for cancer research in memory of my father."

Keith Brackney—Brackney's Western Store, Greencastle

Boil **1 small POTATO** approximately the size of a large egg. Mash the potato and then knead in **1 pound of POWDERED SUGAR.** Flavor with **VANILLA.** Roll out to a 1/8-inch thick rectangle and spread with **PEANUT BUTTER.** Roll up and slice like a jelly roll.

Variation: Make into balls and roll in **COCONUT** and/or **chopped NUTS.**

5 - 3 - 2 Icing

"This is my mother-in-law's recipe. The origin is unknown, but I feel it is quite old."

Mary E. Gifford—Lebanon

5 Tbsp. BROWN SUGAR
3 Tbsp. BUTTER

2 Tbsp. BOILING WATER
POWDERED SUGAR

In a small saucepan, mix brown sugar, butter and water together and bring to a boil. Let cool then thicken with powdered sugar to desired consistency.

Devil's Food Cake with Caramel Icing

"This is a fourth generation recipe passed down from my great-grandmother, May Flint."

Keith Brackney—Brackney's Western Store, Greencastle

1/3 cup COCOA
1/2 cup BOILING WATER
1 tsp. BAKING SODA
1/2 cup SOUR MILK*
1 cup packed BROWN SUGAR

1 cup SUGAR
2 EGGS
1/2 cup BUTTER
2 1/2 cups FLOUR
1 tsp. VANILLA

Preheat oven to 375°. Dissolve cocoa in boiling water. Stir baking soda into the milk. In a large bowl, mix all ingredients together and beat well. Pour batter into two greased and floured 9-inch layer pans and bake for 30 minutes or until tests done. When cool, spread with *Caramel Icing.*

*Sour milk can be made by combining 1 1/2 tsp. lemon juice, plus enough milk to equal 1/2 cup. Let stand for 5 minutes.

Caramel Icing

2 cups packed BROWN SUGAR　　**1/2 cup HEAVY CREAM**

Place sugar and cream in the top of a double boiler and cook to soft ball stage. Cool; beat until thick enough to spread.

Nut Strudel

"This recipe was given to me by my favorite aunt years ago. A Christmas hasn't gone by without it. I like to color and decorate the icing to go with the holiday. It is a great dessert for special occasions, too."

Laura McInturf—Elkhart

1 box PILLSBURY® HOT ROLL MIX
1/2 lb. MARGARINE or BUTTER, melted
1 bag (16 oz.) WALNUTS, finely crushed
1 3/4 cups SUGAR

Preheat oven to 350°. Prepare hot roll mix, allowing it to rise only once. Roll dough out into a 1/8-inch thick circle. Spread 3/4 of the margarine onto the dough. In a small bowl, combine nuts and sugar and mix thoroughly. Spread mixture on dough to within 1/8-inch of the edge. Starting with the edge closest to you, roll the dough away from you into a semi-tight cylinder. Place dough on a greased, round pizza pan, tucking one end into the other. Flatten with hand to about 2-inches high; spread remaining margarine on top. Bake for 20 minutes or until golden brown. Spread with ***Powdered Sugar Icing***.

Powdered Sugar Icing

1/2 tsp. BUTTER   1/2 tsp. VANILLA
2 Tbsp. HOT MILK   1 1/2 cups POWDERED SUGAR

In a bowl, dissolve butter in milk; add vanilla and then slowly stir in enough powdered sugar to reach spreading consistency.

Just What Does "Hoosier" Mean?

One popular theory suggests that when a pioneer visitor knocked on a cabin door, the settler would respond, "Who's yere?" And from this, Indiana became the "Hoosier" state. Another states that there was a contractor named Hoosier employed on the Louisville and Portland Canal who preferred to hire laborers from Indiana. They were called "Hoosier's men" hence, the state's nickname, "Hoosier."

Apricot-Pineapple Pie

"This pie was my mother's favorite for family dinners and church suppers. My mother won Grand Champion for her pie at the Indiana State Fair for 2 years. She never had a written 'recipe', so I worked out my own."

Madonna Alderson—Sharpsville

1 can (17 oz.) APRICOTS, chopped
1 can (20 oz.) CRUSHED PINEAPPLE
1 cup SUGAR
3 Tbsp. CORNSTARCH
1 Tbsp. TAPIOCA

2 Tbsp. BUTTER
1 tsp. LEMON JUICE

Preheat oven to 450°. Drain fruit, combine juices and measure 3/4 cup. In a saucepan, combine sugar, cornstarch, tapioca and juice mixture. Cook until thickened. Stir in butter, lemon juice and fruit and cook for an additional 5 minutes. Pour into *Pie Crust.* Add top crust and bake at 450° for 15 minutes, then reduce heat to 250° and bake for an additional 45 minutes.

Pie Crust

3 cups FLOUR
1 tsp. SALT
1 cup SHORTENING

5-6 Tbsp. WATER
1 EGG
1 Tbsp. LEMON JUICE

In a mixing bowl, combine flour and salt; cut in shortening until mixture resembles a coarse meal. In a small bowl, combine water, egg and lemon juice and beat well. Gently work small amounts of the liquid into the flour mixture until dough clings together when pressed into a ball. Roll out 1/2 of the dough to 1/8-inch thickness and fit into a 9-inch pie pan. Roll out remaining dough and cut into strips for lattice-style top.

Shipshewana

This northern Indiana city is home to one of the largest Amish communities in the world. The city was named after Chief Shipshewana of the Potawatomi Indian Tribe.

Grandma Snyder's Butterscotch Cookies

"These cookies were our family favorites! My grandpa always dipped his cookies in his coffee. It seemed we always had homemade cookies in the cookie jar and loved to sneak them while 'Grams' was busy elsewhere."

Glenna Brown—Auburn

1/2 cup BUTTER
2 cups packed BROWN
    SUGAR
2 EGGS, beaten

3 1/2 cups FLOUR
1 tsp. CREAM OF TARTAR
1 tsp. BAKING SODA
5 tsp. MILK

In a large mixing bowl, cream butter and sugar together until smooth. Add eggs and mix well. Sift flour, cream of tartar and baking soda together and add to creamed mixture alternating with the milk; blend well. Form dough into a 2-inch roll, wrap in waxed paper and refrigerate overnight. Slice dough into 1/4-inch thick slices and place on cookie sheet. Bake at 350° for 8-12 minutes or until golden brown.

Note: Add more flour for a firmer cookie.

Golden Pineapple Dessert

"This is an easy dessert to make that everyone will enjoy. It is especially good served with ice cream."

Darlene Hyndman—Fort Wayne

2 cans (20 oz. ea.) PINEAPPLE CHUNKS
1 1/2 cups SUGAR
1 stick MARGARINE
8 slices WHITE BREAD, torn into small pieces

Drain pineapple juice into a saucepan and add sugar and margarine; bring mixture to a boil. Arrange pineapple chunks in a greased 13 x 9 glass baking dish. Layer bread on top of pineapple. Pour juice mixture over bread, soaking each piece. Bake at 325° for 40 minutes or until light golden brown.

Apple Dapple Cake

"A family favorite. It never lasts very long when I bake it!"

Marietta Eastlund—Plymouth

2 cups SUGAR	2 cups chopped PECANS
1 1/2 cups VEGETABLE OIL	3 cups chopped GRANNY
3 EGGS	SMITH APPLES
2 cups FLOUR	
1 tsp. SALT	Topping:
1 tsp. BAKING SODA	1 1/2 tsp. CINNAMON
1 tsp. CINNAMON	1/2 cup SUGAR
1 tsp. VANILLA	1/2 cup chopped PECANS

Pre-heat oven to 300°. Cream sugar and oil thoroughly, add eggs and beat well. Sift flour, salt, baking soda and cinnamon together and blend into egg mixture. Add vanilla and mix well. Fold in nuts and apples. In a bowl, combine topping ingredients. Pour cake batter into a lightly greased 12 x 9 baking pan. Sprinkle topping mixture evenly over batter. Bake for 1 hour or until cake tests done.

Clarksville

The 950 acre Falls of the Ohio State Park, near Clarksville, contains a huge fossil bed of coral and prehistoric ocean life more than 400 million years old.

Persimmon Pudding

"This family favorite uses a fruit native to our state."

Imogene Stanley—Clarksville

1 cup FLOUR	1 tsp. CINNAMON
1 cup PERSIMMON PULP	1 tsp. BAKING SODA
1 cup SUGAR	1/4 tsp. SALT
1 cup BUTTERMILK	1/2 cup BUTTER, melted
1 EGG, beaten	and cooled

In a large mixing bowl, combine all ingredients except butter and mix well. Stir in butter. Pour into a buttered 9 x 9 cake pan. Bake at 350° for 1 hour or until top is golden brown.

Cinnamon Pudding

"This is a family recipe from Amish heritage."

Rosannah E. Shaw—Elkhart

2 cups packed BROWN SUGAR	1 cup SUGAR
1 1/2 cups COLD WATER	1 cup MILK
4 Tbsp. BUTTER, divided	2 tsp. CINNAMON
2 cups FLOUR	1/2 tsp. SALT
2 tsp. BAKING POWDER	1/2 cup chopped NUTS
	8 oz. WHIPPED TOPPING

In a saucepan, combine brown sugar, water and 2 tablespoons of butter; bring to a boil and cook until thickened. In a large mixing bowl, stir together flour, baking powder, sugar, milk, cinnamon, salt and remaining butter. Pour into a greased 13 x 9 pan then pour brown sugar mixture over the top. Sprinkle with nuts. Bake at 350° for 25-30 minutes. Cool to lukewarm; blend in whipped topping and serve.

Did You Know?
In 1911, the first 500-mile Memorial Day automobile race was held in Indianapolis.

Autumn Grape Pie

"This recipe has been a favorite in my family for over 50 years."

Marian Miller—Michigan City

5 1/2 cups CONCORD GRAPES	Dash of SALT
1 1/2 cups SUGAR	1 1/3 Tbsp. BUTTER
4 Tbsp. FLOUR	2 (9-inch) unbaked PIE SHELLS
1 1/2 tsp. LEMON JUICE	

Remove grape skins and reserve. Place pulp in a saucepan (do not add water) and bring to a rolling boil. While pulp is hot, rub through a strainer to remove seeds. Combine strained pulp with skins, sugar, flour, lemon juice and salt. Pour mixture into pie shell and dot top with butter. Add top pie shell and prick with a fork to ventilate. Bake for 45 minutes in a 400° oven.

Grandma's
Strawberry-Rhubarb Pie

"My great-grandmother, Elizabeth Zulich, was well-known in Porter County for her cooking, and when it came to pies, no one could come close!"

Anne-Marie Buibish—Churubusco

6 cups FLOUR	1 cup + 2 Tbsp. ICE WATER
1 tsp. SALT	2 Tbsp. MILK
1 lb. SHORTENING	1 Tbsp. SUGAR
2 Tbsp. VINEGAR	

Preheat oven to 350°. In a large mixing bowl, combine flour and salt and mix well; cut in shortening until mixture forms coarse crumbs. Mix vinegar with water and sprinkle over flour mixture. Mix lightly just until dough holds together when pressed into a ball. Roll out 1/2 of the dough to 1/4-inch thickness and a few inches larger than a 9-inch pie pan, then fit the dough loosely into pie pan. Pour in ***Strawberry-Rhubarb Filling***. Roll out remaining dough, cut several small vent openings, then drape on top of filling. Crimp the bottom and top crusts together. Brush lightly with milk and sprinkle with sugar. Bake for 1 hour.

Strawberry-Rhubarb Filling

1 cup SUGAR	1 1/2 cups fresh RHUBARB,
3 Tbsp. FLOUR	cut into 1/2-inch pieces
Pinch of SALT	1 Tbsp. LEMON JUICE
1 1/2 cups fresh	1 Tbsp. WATER
STRAWBERRIES	1 Tbsp. BUTTER

In a large mixing bowl, combine sugar, flour and salt. Toss in strawberries, rhubarb, lemon juice and water. Place fruit mixture into pie crust and dot with butter.

Shoofly Pie

"The shoofly pie, in its original form of a sponge cake baked in a crust, came from Pennsylvania Dutch ovens. Its sweet ingredients ensured its popularity among flies, hence the name."

Angie Pletcher Stillson—Amish Acres, Nappanee

1 1/4 cups FLOUR
1/2 cup packed BROWN SUGAR
1/2 tsp. CINNAMON
1/4 tsp. SALT
3 Tbsp. VEGETABLE OIL
1/2 tsp. BAKING SODA

3/4 cup BOILING WATER
1/2 cup DARK CORN SYRUP
1/4 cup LIGHT MOLASSES
1 EGG, well-beaten
1 (9-inch) unbaked PIE
   SHELL

In a bowl, combine flour, sugar, cinnamon and salt. Blend in oil and set aside. Dissolve baking soda in boiling water. Stir in corn syrup and molasses. Let mixture cool. Add egg. Sprinkle 1/2 cup of flour mixture into pie shell. Carefully cover with liquid filling. Top with remaining flour mixture. Bake at 375° for 25-30 minutes or until mixture sets.

Hickory Nut Cream Cake

"Cream was readily available for most farm wives. They could just go to the milk house and dip the cream off the top of a can of milk. The cream in this recipe replaces the lard that was used in the past and gives this cake a delightful flavor."

Jeanne Flanders—Flanders A-Maizing Grain, Inc., Noblesville

2 EGGS, beaten
2 cups SUGAR
2 cups WHIPPING CREAM
4 cups FLOUR

4 tsp. BAKING POWDER
2 tsp. VANILLA
1 cup chopped HICKORY
   NUTS

In a large bowl, combine eggs and sugar and beat well. Add cream and beat lightly. Sift flour and baking powder together, stir into creamed mixture and mix until smooth. Stir in vanilla and nuts. Pour into two greased 9-inch round cake pans. Bake at 350° for 30 minutes or until toothpick inserted in center comes out clean.

Bowery Pie

"This delicious pie was served at the former Tea Room located on Bower Street. It is a delightful treat for pecan and chocolate lovers and a popular choice at the Trolley Cafe."

Aaron and Mary Jane Hoober—Trolley Cafe, Goshen

4 oz. CHOCOLATE BITS or
    MILK CHOCOLATE SQUARES
1 (9-inch) unbaked PIE SHELL
1 cup LIGHT CORN SYRUP
3 EGGS

1 cup packed BROWN
    SUGAR
1/3 cup BUTTER, melted
1 1/2 cups PECANS

Place chocolate on bottom of pie shell. In a medium mixing bowl, blend together corn syrup, eggs, brown sugar and butter; stir in pecans. Pour mixture on top of chocolate. Bake at 350° for 45 minutes or until pie is set.

Touchdown Popcorn Medley

4 qts. POPCORN
1 cup UNSALTED PEANUTS
1 cup SEEDLESS RAISINS
1 cup HONEY
1/2 cup WATER
1 Tbsp. LEMON JUICE

Preheat oven to 300°. In a large buttered bowl, mix together popcorn, peanuts and raisins. In a saucepan, combine honey, water and lemon juice. Bring to a boil; cook and stir over medium heat until mixture reaches hard ball stage or 250° on a candy thermometer. Pour mixture over popcorn; toss to mix thoroughly. Turn onto a buttered jelly roll pan or large baking pan. Bake for 20 minutes, stirring occasionally.

Did You Know?
Indiana has produced more popcorn than any other state or nation.

Caramel Corn

10 cups POPCORN	1/2 tsp. SALT
1/2 cup MARGARINE	1/2 cup LIGHT CORN SYRUP
1 cup packed BROWN SUGAR	1/2 tsp. BAKING POWDER

Place popcorn in a large bowl. In a saucepan over medium heat, melt margarine. Add brown sugar, salt and corn syrup. Mix thoroughly and remove from heat. Add baking powder and mix well. Pour over popcorn and toss to coat.

Rhubarb Dumplings

"My Amish grandmother gave me this recipe. I added the diced apple to cut back on sugar."

Ruth Ann Mast—Bremen

2 cups FLOUR	1/2 cup SUGAR
2 tsp. BAKING POWDER	3 cups finely chopped
1 tsp. SALT	RHUBARB
2 1/2 Tbsp. SHORTENING	1 med. APPLE, peeled,
7/8 cup MILK	cored and chopped
1/3 cup BUTTER, softened	3/4-1 tsp. grated NUTMEG

In a large mixing bowl, sift together flour, baking powder and salt; cut in shortening. Add milk and mix well. Roll dough out to a 15 x 11 rectangle. Spread butter over surface of dough and sprinkle with sugar. Arrange rhubarb and apple on top of sugar; sprinkle with nutmeg. Roll up like a jelly roll, starting at the longest end, then cut into 1 1/2 to 2-inch slices. Place slices in a greased 13 x 9 pan. Pour **Sweet Sauce** over and around dumplings. Bake at 350° for 35-40 minutes or until browned.

Sweet Sauce

1 heaping Tbsp. FLOUR	1 cup HOT WATER
1/4 tsp. SALT	3 Tbsp. BUTTER
1 cup SUGAR	1/2-3/4 tsp. grated NUTMEG

In a saucepan, whisk flour and salt into sugar. Whisk in hot water until mixture is smooth; stir in butter and nutmeg. Bring mixture to a boil over medium heat and cook for 3 minutes.

Zucchini Cake

"This is one of my favorite recipes."

Lena A. France—Noblesville

1 1/2 cups OIL
3 cups SUGAR
4 EGGS, well-beaten
3 cups grated ZUCCHINI

3 cups FLOUR
1 Tbsp. BAKING SODA
2 Tbsp. BAKING POWDER
1 1/2 Tbsp. CINNAMON

Icing:
1 box (16 oz.) POWDERED SUGAR
8 oz. CREAM CHEESE, softened
1/2 stick MARGARINE, softened

Preheat oven to 300°. In a large mixing bowl, combine oil, sugar, and eggs and mix well; stir in zucchini. Add flour, baking soda, baking powder and cinnamon. Pour batter into two 9-inch round cake pans and bake for 1 hour or until toothpick inserted in center comes out clean. In a medium bowl, beat together powdered sugar, cream cheese and margarine until smooth. When cake has thoroughly cooled, add icing.

Mom's Magic Peach Cobbler

"My mother goes to southern Indiana to pick peaches every year, then she prepares them for the freezer. This is our family's favorite dessert. It's very quick to make and delicious!"

Dotti Thomas—Frankfort

1 stick BUTTER
2 cups SUGAR, divided
1 cup FLOUR

1 1/2 tsp. BAKING POWDER
3/4 cup MILK
2 cups sliced PEACHES

Melt butter in a 13 x 9 baking dish. In a medium bowl, combine 1 cup of sugar, flour, baking powder and milk; mix well. Pour batter evenly over the melted butter; do not stir. Top with peach slices and sprinkle with remaining sugar. Bake at 350° for 30 minutes.

Old-Fashioned Suet Pudding

"This steamed pudding recipe was a personal favorite and rare treat while growing up. It was passed down from my paternal grandmother who was of German descent; I believe the recipe came to her from my Grandfather Vernon's family. My ancestor, Admiral Edward Vernon (Old Groggy), was a commander in the British Navy. It is said that George Washington's home, Mount Vernon, was named after him."

Mary E. Gifford—Lebanon

1 tsp. BAKING SODA	1 cup FLOUR
1/4 cup HOT WATER	1 cup RAISINS
1 cup SUET, diced	1 cup MILK
1 cup SUGAR	2 cups BREAD CRUMBS

Sauce:

2 EGGS, beaten	2 Tbsp. VINEGAR
1 cup SUGAR	2 cups BOILING WATER
1/2 cup BUTTER	1 tsp. VANILLA

In a small bowl, dissolve baking soda in hot water. In a large mixing bowl, combine all pudding ingredients and mix thoroughly. Pour mixture into a pudding basin or coffee can so that mixture only fills container to three-quarters capacity. Cover tightly with aluminum foil and stand on a rack in a pan of boiling water with water extending at least halfway up the basin or can. Steam for 3 hours. In a saucepan, combine all sauce ingredients and mix well. Cook until thickened. Place servings on plates or in bowls and top with warm sauce.

Rome City

This city began as an encampment of laborers working on an Elkhart River dam in 1837. When the workers complained about bad living conditions, they were told, "do as the Romans do," thus they named their collection of shacks Rome. Later residents changed the name to Rome City.

Yellow Angel Food Cake

"This is a very old recipe. My mom baked this cake many years ago and now my sisters and I bake it. It is so good and moist too!"

Marie Martin—Greensburg

1 1/2 cups FLOUR	Pinch of SALT
1 tsp. BAKING POWDER	1/2 cup COLD WATER
5 EGGS, separated	1 1/2 cups SUGAR
3/4 tsp. CREAM OF TARTAR	1 tsp. VANILLA

Sift flour and baking powder 5 times into a bowl. In another bowl, beat egg whites with cream of tartar and salt until stiff. Place egg yolks in a large mixer bowl, add water and beat at medium speed until fluffy; add sugar and beat well. Add flour mixture and vanilla and beat well; fold in egg whites. Pour into an angel food cake pan. Bake at 300° for 1 hour, remove and allow to cool. Drizzle with a thin powdered sugar icing.

Did You Know?

The East Race Waterway in South Bend is one of only a few man-made white-water courses in the world.

Beer Cake

"This is my grandmother's recipe and has been a family favorite for years."

James F. Erlacher—Elkhart

2 cups packed DARK BROWN SUGAR	2 cups BEER
2 tsp. BAKING SODA	3 cups FLOUR
1 cup BUTTER or MARGARINE	1 tsp. SALT
2 EGGS	1 tsp. CLOVES
1 1/2 cups chopped NUTS	1 tsp. CINNAMON
2 cups chopped DATES	1 tsp. ALLSPICE

In a bowl, cream together sugar, baking soda and butter. Add eggs and beat until smooth. Fold in nuts and dates alternately with beer. Sift flour and seasonings together, then stir into batter. Mix well. Pour batter into a greased and floured tube pan. Bake at 300° for 1 1/2 hours or until tests done.

Potato Doughnuts

"This is my mother's recipe and it is very good!"

Bonnie L. Domer—Bristol

2 cups MASHED POTATOES	2 tsp. BAKING POWDER
2 1/2 cups SUGAR	1 tsp. NUTMEG
2 cups BUTTERMILK	1/2 tsp. SALT
2 EGGS, lightly beaten	6 1/2-7 cups FLOUR
2 Tbsp. BUTTER, melted	VEGETABLE OIL for frying
2 tsp. BAKING SODA	

In a large mixing bowl, combine potatoes, sugar, buttermilk and eggs and mix well. Stir in butter, baking soda, baking powder, nutmeg, salt and enough flour to form a soft dough. Turn dough out onto a lightly floured surface and knead until smooth. Pat out to 3/4-inch thickness and cut with a 2 1/2-inch floured doughnut cutter. In a heavy skillet, heat 1 inch of oil to 375°. Fry doughnuts for 2 minutes on each side or until brown; drain on paper towels. Top with your favorite frosting.

Makes 4 dozen doughnuts.

Momma's
Peanut Butter Fudge

"My mother, Mary Maxine Corbin, worked at the RCA plant in Bloomington for many years. This is a recipe that she acquired from a fellow worker at the plant. It is a 'must have' at all of our family gatherings."

Sharon Wilson—Kati-Scarlett Bed & Breakfast, Lapel

3 cups SUGAR	1 tsp. VANILLA
1 can EVAPORATED MILK	1 jar (18 oz.) CREAMY
Dash of SALT	PEANUT BUTTER
2 Tbsp. BUTTER	

Place sugar, evaporated milk and salt in a saucepan. Cook to soft ball stage. Remove pan from heat. Add remaining ingredients and beat with a mixer until stiff. Pour into a 9 x 9 baking pan and cut into squares before fudge hardens.

Old Tippecanoe Cake

This cake is sometimes called Harrison Cake in honor of William Henry Harrison and is said to have been his favorite. This recipe, believed to be of New England origin, was used in the White House during his administration.

Grouseland, William Henry Harrison Mansion—Vincennes

1 1/2 cups BUTTER	2 Tbsp. CINNAMON
1 1/2 cups SUGAR	1 Tbsp. CLOVES
3 EGGS, well-beaten	2 Tbsp. ALLSPICE
1 1/2 cups DARK MOLASSES	1 1/4 cups MILK
or SORGHUM	1 lb. SEEDLESS RAISINS
4 oz. BRANDY or WINE	1 lb. CURRANTS
6 cups FLOUR	1/4 lb. CITRON, diced
1 tsp. BAKING SODA	1 Tbsp. LEMON JUICE
2 Tbsp. MACE	

Cream butter and sugar together. Stir in eggs, molasses and brandy. Sift together flour, baking soda, and spices; add to creamed mixture, alternating with milk. Stir in remaining ingredients and mix thoroughly. Pour into a well-greased, well-lined (brown paper, then waxed paper) 13 x 9 baking pan. Bake for 2 1/2 hours at 325°. When done, cover with cloth that has been dipped in brandy, wrap in waxed paper and foil. Cake will keep for months and improves with age.

Aunt Katie's Cream Cake

"When I was a young child recuperating from an accident, my Aunt Katie sent this cake to cheer me up."

Betty J. Richardson—Lebanon

2 EGGS	1 cup SUGAR
CREAM	1 tsp. VANILLA
1 1/2 cups FLOUR	1 tsp. BAKING POWDER

Break eggs into a measuring cup then fill to one cup with cream. Place egg mixture in a bowl and combine with remaining ingredients. Beat well. Pour batter into a greased 13 x 9 baking pan. Bake at 350° for 30 minutes or until tests done.

Indiana Food Festival Sampler

March—**Parke County Maple Syrup Festival**—Rockville.

April—**Mansfield Mushroom Festival**—Mansfield. **Redbud Trail Rendezvous**—Rochester.

May—**Elwood Spring Festival**—Elwood. **Fiesta Cinco de Mayo**—Warsaw. **Mentone Egg Festival**—Mentone.

June—**All American Hoe-Down Festival**—Campbellsburg. **All American Picnic**—Portage. **Blue Jeans Festival**—Rising Sun. **Heritage Lake Summerfest**—Fillmore. **Middle Eastern Festival**—Indianapolis. **Mint Festival**—North Judson. **Newburgh Summer Fest**—Newburgh. **Round Barn Festival**—Rochester. **South Bend Ethnic Festival**—South Bend. **Very Berry Strawberry Fest**—Wabash. **Wabash Valley Summer Festival**—Geneva. **Westfield Summer Fest**—Westfield. **Strawberry Festival**—Crawfordsville.

July—**Bass Lake Summer Splash**—Knox. **Circus City Festival**—Peru. **City of Lakes Festival**—Warsaw. **Frankfort Hot Dog Festival**—Frankfort. **Gaelic Fest**—Valparaiso. **Kosciusko County 4-H Fair**—Warsaw. **Pierogi Festival**—Whiting. **Swiss Days**—Berne. **Three Rivers Festival**—Fort Wayne. **Raspberry Fest**—Batesville.

August—**Farmersburg Festival**—Farmersburg. **Harvest Festival**—Knox. **Medaryville Community Potato Fest**—Medaryville. **Monroeville Harvest Fest**—Monroeville. **Riverboat Days**—Rising Sun. **Sweet Corn Festival**—Oakland. **Swiss Wine Festival**—Vevay. **VanBuren Popcorn Festival**—VanBuren. **Knox County Watermelon Festival**—Vincennes.

September—**Plymouth Blueberry Festival**—Plymouth. **Fall Creek Heritage Fair**—Pendleton. **Indianapolis Greek Festival**—Indianapolis. **International Culture Festival**—Hammond. **Indiana Summer Festival**—Paoli. **Persimmon Festival**—Mitchell. **Rush County Festival**—Rushville. **Scotland Festival**—Scotland. **Terre Haute Annual Ethnic Festival**—Terre Haute. **Tipton County Pork Festival**—Tipton. **Valparaiso Popcorn Festival**—Valparaiso. **Apple Fest**—Batesville. **Berne Heritage Festival**—Berne. **Taste of Tippecanoe**—Lafayette.

October—**Amish Country Harvest Festival**—Middlebury. **Apple Festival of Kendallville**—Kendallville. **Covington Apple Festival**—Covington. **Elwood Chili Cook-Off**—Elwood. **Feast of the Hunters Moon**—Lafayette. **Harvest Moon Festival**—Sheridan. **Heartland Apple Festival**—Danville. **Navy Bean Festival**—Rising Sun. **North Manchester Harvest Festival**—North Manchester. **Riley Festival**—Greenfield. **Seymour Octoberfest**—Seymour. **Sunset Hills Fall Farm Festival**—Valparaiso. **County Pumpkin Festival**—French Lick. **Stumler Applefest**—Starlight.

Index

Index (continued)

Index (continued)

Index (continued)

Indiana Cook Book Contributors

Cooking Across America Cook Book Series™

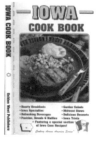

IOWA COOK BOOK

Recipes from across America's heartland. From *Indian Two-Corn Pudding* to *Pork Chops Braised in White Wine* this cookbook presents home-grown favorites and encompasses both ethnic traditions and gourmet specialties. A section entitled "Iowa Corn Recipes" highlights this state's most famous export.

5 1/2 x 8 1/2 — 96 pages . . . $6.95

ILLINOIS COOK BOOK

Enjoy the flavors of Illinois! Over 100 recipes that celebrate Illinois. *Reuben in the Round, Pork Medallions in Herb Sauce, Autumn's Swiss Supper, Carrot Soufflé, Sky High Honey Biscuits* and *Rhubarb Cream Pie*, to name just a few. Includes fascinating facts and trivia.

5 1/2 x 8 1/2 — 96 pages . . . $6.95

MINNESOTA COOK BOOK

Featuring Minnesota's rich blend of cultures and culinary traditions. Eye-opening breakfast and brunch selections, distinctive soup and salad recipes, savory main and side dishes and delicious desserts. From *Zucchini Pancakes* to *Swedish Almond Rusks,* you'll find recipes for every occasion!

5 1/2 x 8 1/2 — 96 pages . . . $6.95

WISCONSIN COOK BOOK

Favorite Old World, regional and contemporary recipes from the best cooks throughout Wisconsin! Delicious recipes for Wisconsin's bountiful fruit, fresh produce, wild game, fish and fowl. Plus fascinating historical and state trivia!

5 1/2 x 8 1/2 — 112 pages . . . $6.95

KANSAS COOK BOOK

Over 125 luscious recipes capture the rich cultural and histori-cal charm of Kansas. Traditional and contemporary recipes include favorites such as *Pumpkin Dumplin's with Apple Chutney, Sunflower Salad, Kansas Beef Strogonoff, Corn Fritters* and *Yellow Brick Road Cake.* Entertaining Kansas trivia and facts.

5 1/2 x 8 1/2 — 96 pages . . . $6.95

APPLE LOVERS COOK BOOK

Celebrating America's favorite—the apple! 150 recipes for main and side dishes, appetizers, salads, breads, muffins, cakes, pies, desserts, beverages and preserves, all kitchen-tested by Shirley Munson and Jo Nelson.

5 1/2 x 8 1/2 — 120 Pages . . . $6.95

BERRY LOVERS COOK BOOK

Berrylicious recipes for enjoying these natural wonders. From *Blueberry Muffins, Strawberry Cheesecake* and *Raspberry Sticky Rolls* to *Boysenberry Mint Frosty* or *Gooseberry Crunch,* you will find tasty recipes that will bring raves from your friends and family. Includes berry facts and trivia.

5 1/2 x 8 1/2 — 96 Pages . . . $6.95

VEGGIE LOVERS COOK BOOK

Everyone will love these no-cholesterol, no-animal recipes! Over 200 nutritious, flavorful recipes by Chef Morty Star. Includes a foreword by Dr. Michael Klaper. Nutritional analysis for each recipe to help you plan a healthy diet.

5 1/2 x 8 1/2 — 128 pages . . . $6.95

BEST BARBECUE RECIPES

A collection of more than 200 taste-tempting recipes. • Sauces • Marinades • Rubs • Mops • Ribs • Wild Game • Fish and Seafood • Pit barbecue and more! By Mildred Fischer.

5 1/2 x 8 1/2—144 pages . . . $5.95

CORN LOVERS COOK BOOK

Over 100 delicious recipes featuring America's favorite! Try *Corn Chowder, Corn Soufflé, Apple Cornbread* or *Caramel Corn,* to name a few. You will find a tempting recipe for every occasion in this collection. Includes corn facts and trivia, too!

5 1/2 x 8 1/2 — 88 pages . . . $6.95

ORDER BLANK

GOLDEN WEST PUBLISHERS

 4113 N. Longview Ave. • Phoenix, AZ 85014

www.goldenwestpublishers.com • **1-800-658-5830** • FAX 602-279-6901

Qty	Title	Price	Amount
	Apple Lovers Cook Book	6.95	
	Bean Lovers Cook Book	6.95	
	Berry Lovers Cook Book	6.95	
	Best Barbecue Recipes	5.95	
	Chili-Lovers' Cook Book	5.95	
	Chip and Dip Lovers Cook Book	5.95	
	Corn Lovers Cook Book	6.95	
	Easy Recipes for Wild Game & Fish	6.95	
	Illinois Cook Book	6.95	
	Indiana Cook Book	6.95	
	Iowa Cook Book	6.95	
	Joy of Muffins	5.95	
	Kansas Cook Book	6.95	
	Minnesota Cook Book	6.95	
	Pumpkin Lovers Cook Book	6.95	
	Quick-n-Easy Mexican recipes	5.95	
	Recipes for a Healthy Lifestyle	6.95	
	Salsa Lovers Cook Book	5.95	
	Veggie Lovers Cook Book	6.95	
	Wisconsin Cook Book	6.95	
Shipping & Handling Add ▥▶	U.S. & Canada	$3.00	
	Other countries	$5.00	

☐ My Check or Money Order Enclosed $

☐ MasterCard   ☐ VISA ($20 credit card minimum)

(Payable in U.S. funds)

Acct. No.   Exp. Date

Signature

Name   Telephone

Address

City/State/Zip   **Call for a FREE catalog of all of our titles**   Indiana CkBk
5/01

This order blank may be photocopied.